Lao Zi's Dao De Jing for Nemonik Thinkers

The Way of Nature

and

The Way of People

First Edition

Dr. Auke Schade

nemonik-thinking.org

Copyright

Copyright © September 2016 by Dr. Auke Schade. All rights reserved. This copy of—*Lao Zi's Dao De Jing for Nemonik Thinkers*—is for private use only. This copy or any part thereof shall not be resold, reproduced, or transmitted in any form or by any means, electronic or mechanical, including photocopying, recording, or otherwise, or placed in any public information storage and retrieval system, including the Internet, without a prior written permission from the copyright owner.

First Edition
Published 10 September 2016
@ nemonik-thinking.org
ISBN 978-0-473-37223-1

Abstract

(Schade, Lao Zi's Dao De Jing: Meta-translation, 2016) provides a reliable Chinese-English translation. Nevertheless, *Dao De Jing* has no rational sequence comprising an introduction, main body, and discussion. Even the division of the manuscript in the parts *Dao* and *De* is ambiguous. Topics concerning the *Way of Nature* and the *Way of People* appear almost ad random in the parts *Dao* and *De*. Similar to the notation *Jing*, the division in *Dao* and *De* might have been added later. Lao Zi's unfamiliar format suggests that he used a holistic, rather than a rational approach. He seems to walk around the topic, while telling the reader what he is seeing from different angles. Although that approach enhances the mystery and poetic beauty of that amazing manuscript, it did not produce the most efficient teaching tool. Therefore, I have used the nemonik template to restructure *Dao De Jing* for nemonik thinkers. This template was introduced in (Schade, Think Smarter with Nemonik Thinking, 2016).

nemonik-thinking.org

Dr. Auke Schade

My life started during the devastation of World War II. As a teenager, I worked as a carpenter and studied building engineering at night school. During the seventies, I became a financial manager for a multinational corporation, ran my own business, and studied economics in my spare time. My interest in the psychology of management extended to the interaction between the mind, body, and reality. In 1980, I immigrated to New Zealand where I obtained a doctorate in psychology from the University of Auckland. My mission is to make people the smartest thinkers they can be, which has led me to the development of nemonik thinking.[1]

Download free eBooks and videos
@ nemonik-thinking.org

---

1 Appendix: Nemonik Thinking

Notes

Content

- INTRODUCTION 11
- THE PHYSICS OF PSYCHOLOGY 16
- DAO—THE WAY OF NATURE 17
- PHYSICS 17
    - Reality 18
        - Space 25
        - Matter 25
        - Time 27
- DE—THE WAY OF PEOPLE 29
- PSYCHOLOGY 29
    - Mind 30
        - Conscious 36
        - Rational thinking 36
        - Subconscious 38
        - Affectorial thinking 39
    - Interaction 41
        - Perception 43
        - Projection 46

NEMONIKS 48

Mental nemoniks 48

Objective-1 48

Collective-2 49

Creative-3 59

Reactive-4 60

Operational Nemoniks 65

Advance-5 65

Stay-6 66

Retreat-7 66

Accumulate-8 67

Preserve-9 69

Dispose-10 70

Act-11 72

Wait-12 74

Prepare-13 74

Accept-14 78

Reject-15 78

Reveal-16 80

Conceal-17 81

RESULTS 84
CONCLUSION 87
APPENDICES 93
    Index 94
    Bibliography 111
    List of Tables 113
    Glossary 114
    My Other Books 148
        Lao Zi's Dao De Jing 149
        Lao Tzu's Tao Te Ching 150
        Lao Zi Meta-translation 151
        Lao Zi Explained 152
        Lao Zi Dictionary 153
        Nemonik Thinking 154
        Nemonik Glossary 155
        Nemonik Dictionary 156
        Education Kills Humanity 157
        Global Warming 158
        Sun Zi's The Art of War 159
    Website 160

ENDNOTES 161

INTRODUCTION

A unique translation of Lao Zi's *Dao De Jing* was presented in (Schade, Lao Zi's Dao De Jing: Meta-translation, 2016). Subsequently, his philosophy was explained comprehensively in (Schade, Lao Zi's Dao De Jing Explained, 2016). Nevertheless, Lao Zi's *Dao De Jing* is a holistic manuscript without an introduction, main body, or conclusion. Hence, it is still difficult to read for rational thinkers. Therefore, the current book presents a reorganized version of Lao Zi's manuscript, which is based on the nemonik template that was introduced in (Schade, Think Smarter with Nemonik Thinking, 2016).

```
Nemonik Thinking
    Mind
        Conscious
            Rational thinking
                OBJECTIVE-1
                COLLECTIVE-2
        Subconscious
            Affectorial thinking
                CREATIVE-3
                REACTIVE-4
    Reality
        Space
                ADVANCE-5
                STAY-6
                RETREAT-7
        Matter
                ACCUMULATE-8
                PRESERVE-9
                DISPOSE-10
        Time
                ACT-11
                WAIT-12
                PREPARE-13
    Interaction
        Perception
                ACCEPT-14
                REJECT-15
        Projection
                REVEAL-16
                CONCEAL-17
```

Table 1: Nemonik Template.

Nemonik thinking is the operating system for your mind that you should have received at birth. It is a smarter way of thinking that aims to maximize your success by evaluating seventeen nemoniks, which are memorized keywords describing all the perceived aspects of your mind, reality, and their interaction. In accord with Lao Zi—*Success is obtaining what you seek and escaping what you suffer*. Nemonik thinking is an exhaustive and systematic way of thinking that maximizes the probability of success by subjecting seventeen nemoniks to both rational and affectorial thinking (Schade, Glossary Nemonik Thinking, 2016).

Table 1 shows the nemonik template as introduced in (Schade, Think Smarter with Nemonik Thinking, 2016). In order to facilitate the comparison between that template and Lao Zi's *Dao De Jing* it has to be synchronized with the structure of Lao Zi's manuscript. That manuscript starts with *Dao* or the *Way of Nature*. In nemonik terminology that refers to the laws of nature, physics, and reality. Furthermore, Lao Zi's second part is called *De* or the *Way of People*. In nemonik thinking that refers to psychology, the mind, and the interaction between the mind and reality. In addition, the 17 nemoniks describe the operational options of the mind and, therefore, they are also classified as *De*.

Dao De Jing and nemonik thinking address both the effect of physics on psychology. Nemonik thinking is presented as an exhaustive way of thinking that includes all cognitive possibilities presented by the mind, reality, and their interaction. Therefore, the reorganized *Dao De Jing* should fit within the reorganized nemonik template as shown in Table 2.

Nemonik Thinking		
	Reality	
		Space
		Matter
		Time
	Mind	
		Conscious
		Rational
		Subconscious
		Affectorial
	Interaction	
		Perception
		Projection
	Nemoniks	
		Objective
		Collective
		Creative
		Reactive
		Advance
		Stay
		Retreat
		Accumulate
		Preserve
		Dispose
		Act
		Wait
		Prepare
		Accept
		Reject
		Reveal
		Conceal

Table 2: Nemonik Template for *Dao De Jing*.

Lao Zi's Dao De Jing
老子之道德經

THE PHYSICS OF PSYCHOLOGY

nemonik-thinking.org

DAO—THE WAY OF NATURE

PHYSICS

REALITY

External Reality		
Sensory	Extrasensory	
	Scientific	Supernatural
known	unknown	unknowable
Internal Reality		

Table 3: Diagram of Reality.

External reality—material and immaterial phenomena that surround the mind. The external reality comprises the sensory reality and extrasensory reality. The extrasensory reality comprises the scientific reality and supernatural reality. The subconscious creates the internal, constructed, or simulated reality from the external reality (Schade, Glossary Nemonik Thinking, 2016).

Lao Zi

There was a thing undivided and complete before the Sky and the Earth were born. Desolate. Empty. Independent and unchanging. Yet, it acts as the origin of the world (25). I do not know whose child it is, but it seems to predate the Emperor (4). I do not know how its name is pronounced, but I call it the Way (25). The Way that can be named is not the eternal Way. The name that can be named is not the eternal name (1). The Way is forever nameless (32, 37).

From past to present times, its name was never erased (21). The Way is forever (16). Adhere to the present Way in order to manage the present Existence. Use it to understand its ancient origin. That is called the principle of the Way (14).

The Way generated the One.
The One generated the Two.
The Two generated the Three.
The Three generated All-things (42).

Above the One there is no void. Below it there is no substance. It is infinite. It cannot be named. Every time it returns to Nothingness. It is called shapeless. Like the shape of Nothingness (14). Look at it, yet it cannot be seen. Its name is called invisible. Listen to it, yet it cannot be heard. Its name is called inaudible. Seize it, yet it cannot be caught. Its name is called insubstantial. These three phenomena cannot be extensively evaluated, because they merge into the One (14). Of those in the past that obtained the One: the Sky obtained the One through pureness; the Earth obtained the One through quietness; the mind obtained the One through effectiveness; the valley obtained the One through filling; and Marquises and Kings obtained the One by regulating the world. The conclusion about the One is: if the Sky is not clear yet, then fear that it will crack; if the Earth is not quiet yet, then fear that it will burst; if the mind is not effective yet, then fear that it will cease; and if the valley is not full yet, then fear that it will be dry (39).

The world's things originate from Existence. Existence originates from Non-existence (40). Existence and Non-existence generate each other. Difficult and easy turn into each other. Long and short shape each other. High and low fill each other. Tone and voice harmonise each other. Before and after follow each other forever (2). Thirty spokes merge into one hub, but its Non-existence is useful for a carriage. Moulded clay makes a cup, but the Non-existence of clay is useful for a cup. Chiselled doors and windows make a room, but their Non-existence is useful for a room. Therefore, using Existence is beneficial, while using Non-existence is useful (11).

Music and food will stop passing travellers. However, words describing the Way are called: bland and without taste (35). If I were forced to describe the Way, then I would call it great. Great means continuous. Continuous means forever. Forever means returning. Therefore, the Way is great. The Sky is great. The Earth is great. The King is also great. Inside the Universe there are four Greatnesses and the King is one. Therefore, people follow the Earth, the Earth follows the Sky, the Sky follows the Way, and the Way follows nature (25).

The immortal Valley Spirit is called the Mysterious Female. The home of this Mysterious Female is called the origin of the Sky and the Earth. It seems to exist forever and using it is no hard work (6). The Sky endures and the Earth last long. Why do the Sky and the Earth last long and endure? That is, because they do not foster themselves. Therefore, they can live long (7). The Sky obtained the One through pureness. The Earth obtained the One through quietness (39). If the Sky is not clear yet, then fear that it will crack. If the Earth is not quiet yet, then fear that it will burst (39). If the Sky and the Earth would unite with each other, then it would rain sweet dew (32). What is between the Sky and the Earth is like a bagpipe. It is empty, but not exhausted. Use it and more will be produced (5). After the Way is lost there will be virtue. After virtue is lost, there will be benevolence (38). The Sky and the Earth are not benevolent, because All-things act as straw dogs (5).

Nameless, the Way is the origin of All-things. Being named, it is the Mother of All-things (1). Different names with the same meaning. Profoundly mysterious, they are the gateway to many details (1). People and All-things concentrate on the Way (62). All-things grow without purpose (39). The Way generates them and virtue raises them. The environment shapes them and competence completes them. Therefore, All-things respect the Way and admire virtue (51). The Way generates them and raises them. It grows them and satisfies them. It straightens them and matures them. It supports them and repairs them (51). The Way is empty, but use it and it has not to be refilled. It is so deep! Like the ancestor of All-things: it smooths their blending, untangles their disorder, softens their glare, and merges their dust (4). All-things, grasses, and trees are born soft and fragile. They die, dry and brittle. Therefore, the hard and strong are called companions of death. The soft and weak are the companions of life (76). All-things carry Yin on their back and carry Yang in their arms. Their balance creates vital energy that restores harmony (42).

The Way of nature is like flexing a bow. High things are lowered. Low things are raised. It takes from those who have plenty. It gives to those who have not enough. Therefore, it is the Way of Nature to take from what is plenty and give to what is not enough (77). It is so simple. Yet, the world should not dare to control it (32).

Nature takes a low place. Who knows its reason? The Way of nature is not to strive, but to overcome through competence. Without speaking, it answers with competence. Without calling, things come. It is simple and plans with competence. The net of nature is very extensive. It dredges and nothing escapes (73). Superior goodness is like water. The goodness of water benefits All-things and it does not strive. It occupies places everybody dislikes. Therefore, it is close to the Way (8).

Weakness is used by the Way (40). Nothing in the world is as soft and weak as water. Yet, in attacking hard and strong things, nothing has a greater ability to overcome them. Therefore, nothing could replace its purpose. The softest will overcome the hardest. The weakest will overcome the strongest (78). The softest of the world will overcome the hardest of the world. What is without substance will penetrate what is without gaps (43). Strong things will become weak. They are not called the Way. What is not the Way will soon perish (30, 55).

Returning is the movement of the Way (40). Every time it returns to Nothingness. It is called shapeless. Like the shape of Nothingness (14). The Way is to the world, what a valley is to a river, and what a river is to the sea (32). All-things around us rise, and I watch them return. Those things are numerous and each one returns to its roots. Returning to the roots is called tranquillity. Tranquillity is called returning to order (16). The Way floats. It can be unorthodox or orthodox. It completes its affairs successfully. Yet, it is not a famous being. All-things return to it. Yet, it does not act as their master. It is always without desire. Hence, it could be named small. All-things return to it. Yet, it does not act as their master. Hence, it could be named great (34). Even far away things return to it. The great order is perfect (65).

Look at the Way, yet it cannot be seen. Its name is called invisible. Listen to it, yet it cannot be heard. Its name is called inaudible. Seize it, yet it cannot be caught. Its name is called insubstantial. These three phenomena cannot be extensively evaluated, because they merge into the One (14).

The Way is called shapeless. Like the shape of Nothingness. It is called dim and elusive. Face it, yet you do not see its head. Follow it, yet you do not see its back (14). The contents of the Way are only elusive and dim. Dim. Elusive. Inside there are images. Elusive. Dim. Inside there are things. Tranquil. Obscure. Its centre has energy. Its energy is very real. Inside it, there is information (21). The bright Way seems to be obscure, the Way forward seems to be backwards, and the smooth Way seems to be rough (41). The hidden Way is nameless. Yet, only the Way is good at the beginning and good at the end (41). Look at the Way, and there is not enough to see. Listen to it, and there is not enough to hear. However, use it and it cannot be depleted (35). The Way is empty, but use it and it has not to be refilled. It is so deep (4)!

SPACE

Space—three-dimensional, infinite, and nonmaterial part of reality in which matter is immersed and moves around. Space provides the exhaustive options to *Advance, Stay, and Retreat* (Schade, Glossary Nemonik Thinking, 2016).

Lao Zi

No comments.

MATTER

Matter—three-dimensional finite part of reality that features substance, volume, and weight, and occupies and moves through space and time. Matter is wrapped up energy that is determined by four features: density, volume, shape, and motion. Matter is part of the sensory reality. Matter is organic or inorganic and includes resources such as animals, energy, equipment, information, money, people, plants, raw materials, etc. Einstein's formula $E = mc^2$ shows that energy (E) is another manifestation of matter (m). Information is classified as matter, because there is no information without . Matter provides the exhaustive options to *Accumulate, Preserve, and Dispose* (Schade, Glossary Nemonik Thinking, 2016).

Lao Zi

The world's things originate from Existence. Existence originates from Non-existence (40). Existence and Non-existence generate each other (2). Thirty spokes merge into one hub, but its Non-existence is useful for a carriage. Moulded clay makes a cup, but the Non-existence of clay is useful for a cup. Chiselled doors and windows make a room, but their Non-existence is useful for a room. Therefore, using Existence is beneficial, while using Non-existence is useful (11). Adhere to the present Way in order to manage the present Existence (14).

The Way generated the One. The One generated the Two. The Two generated the Three. The Three generated All-things. All-things carry Yin on their back and carry Yang in their arms. Their balance creates vital energy that restores harmony (42). Inside the Universe there are four Greatnesses and the King is one. Therefore, people follow the Earth, the Earth follows the Sky, the Sky follows the Way, and the Way follows nature (25).

All-things grow without purpose (39). People are born soft and weak. They die, hard and strong. All-things, grasses, and trees are born soft and fragile. They die, dry and brittle. Therefore, the hard and strong are called companions of death. The soft and weak are the companions of life (76).

All-things around us rise, and I watch them return. Those things are numerous and each one returns to its roots (16). All-things return to the Way (34). Like the ancestor of All-things: the Way smooths their blending, untangles their disorder, softens their glare, and merges their dust (4). Sages complement the nature of all All-things, but they do not dare to act (64). All-things rise, but do not initiate them (2).

TIME

Time—one-dimensional, eternal, and nonmaterial part of reality that can be perceived indirectly by changes in matter and the movement of matter through space. Time provides the exhaustive nemoniks to *Act, Wait, and Prepare* (Schade, Glossary Nemonik Thinking, 2016).

Lao Zi

No comments.

Notes

DE—THE WAY OF PEOPLE

PSYCHOLOGY

nemonik-thinking.org

MIND

Mind					
Concentration		Meditation	Relaxation		
Conscious		Semiconscious	Subconscious		
Rational thinking			Affectorial thinking			
Objective	Collective			Creative	Reactive

Table 4: Diagram of the Mind.

Mind—nonmaterial part of a person that comprises the total of all conscious, subconscious, and semiconscious mental structures and processes. The mind is abstract and can only exist in the extrasensory reality, because you cannot see, hear, taste, smell, or touch the mind. The mind is a theoretical construct that exists paradoxically in the mind. Nevertheless, this elusive construct helps us to evaluate our way of thinking. A healthy mind has a will, purpose, or intent that maintains goals such as maximizing success, obtaining comfort, escaping discomfort, and sustaining survival. Furthermore, it has abilities to think and memorize, and to maintain a productive interaction with the external reality (Schade, Glossary Nemonik Thinking, 2016).

Lao Zi

Benefiting life is called fortune. Using the mind's vital energy is called powerful (55). Listening to many details is exhausting and not as good as following your heart (5). In thinking, the goodness is depth (8). Those Ancients who practised the Way competently, understood profoundly the smallest details (15). Why did the Ancients value the protection of the Way of Nature? Did they not say:

Use it to obtain what you seek
and use it to escape what you suffer (62).

Therefore, it is valuable for the whole world (62). The Way of Nature is beneficial and without harm. Accordingly, the Way of People should be action without strive (81).

The Way of Nature has no favourites. It is always with the competent people (79). Those who are courageous in daring will be killed. Those who are courageous in not daring will live (73). Emerging into life is entering into death. Three in ten are companions of life. Three in ten are companions of death. Three in ten people live extremely and move into the realm of death. What is the reason? That is because they live extremely. They are incompetent in hiding, listening, and conserving their lives. Do not walk through the hills in order to meet rhinoceroses and tigers. Do not join the army in order to carry weapons. Rhinoceroses have no place to ram their horns. Tigers have no place to strike their claws. Soldiers have no place to thrust their swords. What is the reason? Because sages avoid the realm of death (50).

People and All-things concentrate on the Way. It is the protection for competent people. It is the sanctuary for incompetent people (62). Incompetent people forsake their existence unnecessarily. Therefore, when the Emperor is crowned and the three ministers are installed, a mill-stone of jade preceded by four horses, is not as good as sitting down and presenting this (62).

The greatest virtue is following only the Way (21). Superior virtue pursues no virtue. Therefore, it is virtue. Inferior virtue pursues virtue. Therefore, it is no virtue (38). Respecting the Way and admiring virtue is not done to obtain a noble position, but it is always done to be natural (51).

From past to present times, its name was never erased. Therefore, align with the Father of the Multitude (21). The beginning of the world is the Mother of the world. Obtain the Mother in order to know her children. When knowing her children, return to their nursing Mother, and life will not be in danger (52). Generate them and raise them. Generate but do not possess. Develop but do not exploit. This is called profound virtue (10). Hold on to the great image, and the world will come. It will come without harm and with great calm. Music and food will stop passing travellers. However, words describing the Way are called: bland and without taste. Look at it, and there is not enough to see. Listen to it, and there is not enough to hear. However, use it and it cannot be depleted (35). The Way is empty, but use it and it has not to be refilled. It is so deep (4)!

Those who submit their affairs to the Way will merge with the Way. Those who submit their affairs to virtue will merge with virtue. Those who submit their affairs to loss will merge with loss. Those who merge with virtue will also gain the Way. Those who merge with loss will also lose the Way (23).

Those who establish it competently cannot be pulled away. Those who embrace it competently cannot be separated. Accordingly, descendants will pay homage forever. Cultivate it in yourself and it will be genuine. Cultivate it in your household and it will be plenty. Cultivate it in your village and its virtue will last long. Cultivate it in your country and its virtue will be abundant. Cultivate it in the world and its virtue will be extensive. Use yourself to examine yourself. Use households to examine households. Use villages to examine villages. Use countries to examine countries. Use the world to examine the world. How do I know that the world is like this? From this account (54).

Competent travellers leave no trail. Competent speakers pursue no flaws. Competent accountants do not use bamboo counting sticks. Competent wardens lock without keys. Yet, it cannot be opened. Competent weavers arrange without strings. Yet, it cannot be untied (27).

Those who have substantial virtue could be compared to new-born babies. Scorpions, vipers, and insects do not bite them. Birds of prey will not seize them. Their bones are weak and their tendons soft. Yet, their grip is firm. They do not know about the joining of male and female. Yet, their male organ is vigorous. Their energy is optimal. They cry all day. Yet, they do not become hoarse. Their harmony is optimal (55). Profound virtue is deep. Even far away things return to it. The great order is perfect (65). Those who overcome other people have power. Those who overcome themselves are strong. Those who know what is enough are rich. Those who are strong pioneers have ambition. Those who do not lose their institutions will last long. Those who die, but are not forgotten, will live on (33).

Everyone in the world calls me great. Great and different. Only those who are different can be great. If they were similar, then they would be insignificant (67). My words are very easy to understand and very easy to apply. Yet, people cannot understand them and they cannot apply them. My words have precedence and my affairs have a sovereign, but they do not understand that. Therefore, they do not understand me. I am valuable to those few who understand me. Therefore, sages wear cheap cloth and conceal jade (70)

Do not leave home in order to learn about the world. Do not look through the window in order to learn about the Way of Nature. The more that people travel far away the less they know. Therefore, sages do not travel and yet they know. They do not see and yet they name. They do not act and yet they achieve (47).

If competent scholars hear about the Way, then they are able to practise it constantly. If mediocre scholars hear about the Way, then they put it in a safe place and seem to lose it. If incompetent scholars hear about the Way, then they laugh loudly about it. If they did not laugh loudly about it, then they could practice the Way. Therefore, an established saying states: *"The bright Way seems to be obscure, the Way forward seems to be backwards, and the smooth Way seems to be rough."* Superior virtue is just like a valley. Great pureness seems to be disgrace. Extensive virtue seems to be insufficient. Established virtue seems to drift along. Plain truth seems to change; the greatest square is without edges; the greatest talent matures late; the greatest sound is a rare tone; and the greatest form is without shape (41). The greatest achievement seems to be incomplete. Yet, its usefulness is not reduced. The greatest fullness seems to be empty. Yet, its usefulness is never exhausted. The greatest straightness seems to bend. The greatest skill seems clumsy. The greatest triumph seems insufficient (45).

CONSCIOUS

Conscious—small part of the mind that is only active when that person is fully awake. The conscious is associated with awareness, concentration, learning, sensory reality, and rational thinking (Schade, Glossary Nemonik Thinking, 2016).

Lao Zi

No comments.

RATIONAL THINKING

Rational thinking—conscious part of nemonik thinking that deals with the predictable order of reality by submitting facts to reason in order to create new facts. Rational thinking uses the mental order of reason to deal with the order of the sensory reality. The mental processes underlying rational thinking are within the conscious awareness, and therefore, they can be observed directly. Rational thinking comprises critical thinking that fosters distrust and emotional detachment. Concentration fosters conscious dominance and rational thinking. Rational thinking comprises the objective and collective mindmodes (Schade, Glossary Nemonik Thinking, 2016).

Lao Zi

Those who know are not educated. Those who are educated do not know (81). Those who know do not speak. Those who speak do not know (56). The more people know, the stranger the things they begin to develop (57).

People are difficult to rule if they use their knowledge. Therefore, using knowledge to rule the country is betraying the country (65). Love the people and rule the country without using knowledge (10). Do not promote the knowledgeable and the people will not strive (3. Let the people be always without knowledge and without desire. Let those who know, not dare to act but stop (3). Discard adoration and reject knowledge and the people will benefit a hundred times (19). Discard knowledge and there are no worries (20).

Knowing that you do not know earns respect. Not knowing that you do not know is a weakness. Therefore, sages are not weak. They consider their weakness as a weakness. Hence, it is not a weakness (71). Those who daily pursue knowledge will expand. Those who daily pursue the Way will contract. Contract and contract until there is Non-action left (48).

SUBCONSCIOUS

Subconscious—large part of the mind that is continuously active outside the conscious awareness of that person. The subconscious is associated with sleep, relaxation, genius, internal reality, and affectorial thinking. The prime aim of the subconscious is to protect the conscious from an information overload. The resulting mental silence allows the conscious to direct and manage the subconscious. The acquisition of information and creation of mindsets cost much time and effort. Therefore, whether correct or incorrect, subconscious information is precious. Consequently, the subconscious has to protect the acquired information against opposing information. However, this protection of the subconscious could cause close mindedness, cognitive dissonance, extremism, groupthink, and mental stagnation. The subconscious generates affectorial thinking (Schade, Glossary Nemonik Thinking, 2016).

Lao Zi

It is not that spirits have no power, but their power will not harm people. Not that power cannot harm people. Sages do not harm people either. Both do not harm each other. Therefore, virtue unites and returns (60).

AFFECTORIAL THINKING

Affectorial thinking—subconscious part of nemonik thinking that deals with the unpredictable chaos of reality by generating affecters that influence the conscious. Affecters are mental signals that are generated by subconscious affectorial thinking, which influence the conscious without explaining the underlying subconscious processes. Affecters include beliefs, desires, discoveries, emotions, fantasies, habits, heuristics, ideas, impulses, innovations, insights, inspirations, intuitions, inventions, novelties, reactions, reflexes, routines, skills, etc. The mental processes underlying affectorial thinking are outside the conscious awareness. Hence, they cannot be observed directly and, therefore, affectorial thinking appears non-rational and irrational to the rational conscious. This is not to say that affectorial thinking is without reason. We just do not know the underlying processes, because they are hidden in the subconscious. The word 'irrational' has often been used as a negative label to discredit affectorial thinking. Furthermore, meditation, relaxation, and a silent mind foster subconscious dominance and affectorial thinking. The opposite of affectorial thinking is rational thinking. Herbert Spencer introduced the unknown and known. These, concepts underlie the division of affectorial thinking into respectively the creative (unknown) and reactive mindmodes (known). Dyslexia and koans might foster affectorial thinking. However, more research is required (Schade, Glossary Nemonik Thinking, 2016).

Lao Zi

Listening to many details is exhausting and not as good as following your heart (5). Those who know other people are wise. Those who know themselves are brilliant (33). Understand the surroundings without using knowledge (10). Do not leave home in order to learn about the world. Do not look through the window in order to learn about the Way of nature. The more that people travel far away the less they know. Therefore, sages do not travel and yet they know. They do not see and yet they name. They do not act and yet they achieve (47).

Knowing harmony is called the constant. Knowing the constant is called brilliance (55). Returning to order is a constant. Knowing this constant is brilliant. Not acknowledging this constant is arrogant. Arrogance causes misfortune. Knowing this constant is embracing. Embracing is honourable. Honourable is Kingly. Kingly is natural. Natural is the Way. The Way is forever. It provides a content life without danger (16). Know the male and guard the female and become the stream of the world (28). Know the white and guard the black and be the example for the world (28). Know the pure and guard the disgrace and be the valley of the world (28). Those who pretend to know the future are the fruitless flowers of the Way and the chiefs of fools. Therefore, great men occupy the thick and do not occupy the thin. Occupy the fruit, but do not occupy the fruitless flowers (38).

INTERACTION

Interaction—effect of the mind on reality and vice versa. Whatever you do affects reality, while reality affects you. Reality is like a mirror that reflects your behaviour, which is called *'karma'*. The exhaustive components of interaction are *Perception* and *Projection* (Schade, Glossary Nemonik Thinking, 2016).

Lao Zi

Flattery and rebuke: how much do they differ from each other (20)? Knowing that you do not know earns respect. Not knowing that you do not know is a weakness. Therefore, sages are not weak. They consider their weakness as a weakness. Hence, it is not a weakness (71). Those who know do not speak. Those who speak do not know (56). Pleasing words might be exchanged. Respectful conduct might honour people (62). True words seem to be paradoxical (78). True words are not pleasing. Pleasing words are not true. Those who know are not educated. Those who are educated do not know (81).

Sages act, but do not rely on it. They succeed, but do not claim. They do not desire to display their knowledge (77). Sages are interfering but not cutting, sharp but not stabbing, straight but not rigid, and bright but not dazzling (58). Sages are always without opinions. They use the opinions of common people as their opinions. They are good to those who are good. They are also good to those who are bad. So they gain goodness. They trust those who trust them. They also trust those who do not trust them. So they gain trustworthiness. Sages depend on the world. Careful, so that they become merged with the opinion of the world. All common people focus their ears and eyes. Instead, all sages are like children (49).

Those Ancients who practised the Way competently, understood profoundly the smallest details. Their depth cannot be known. They cannot be understood. Therefore, they are difficult to describe and called: *"Careful, like they were wading through a river in the winter. Hesitant, like they were afraid of their surrounding neighbours. Solemn, like they were guests. Dissipating, like they were melting snow. Vague, like they were simple. Empty, like they were a valley. Merging, like they were mud"* (15).

Those who wear embroidered coloured silk, carry sharp swords, gorge on food, and have a surplus of goods and resources, are called 'boasting thieves'. Boasting thieves are not the Way (53). Sages who desire to be above the people must place themselves below them. Those who desire to lead people must place themselves behind them. Therefore, they stay above and the people will not weight them down. They stay in front and the people will not harm them. Everyone in the world will be happy to elect them without objection. Having no purpose, they do not strive. Therefore the world cannot strive with them (66). I do not dare to act as a host, but act as a guest. I do not dare to advance an inch, but retreat a foot (69). Show modesty and embrace simplicity. Lack selfishness and restrain desires (19).

PERCEPTION

Perception—part of the nemonik interaction that manages the incoming information flow from the sensory reality towards the mind. The senses facilitate sensory perception by detecting incoming information. The exhaustive options provided by perception for maximizing success are to *Accept and Reject* information (Schade, Glossary Nemonik Thinking, 2016).

Lao Zi

Look at the Way, yet it cannot be seen. Its name is called invisible. Listen to it, yet it cannot be heard. Its name is called inaudible. Seize it, yet it cannot be caught. Its name is called insubstantial. These three phenomena cannot be extensively evaluated, because they merge into the One. Above the One there is no void. Below it there is no substance. It is infinite. It cannot be named. Every time it returns to Nothingness. It is called shapeless. Like the shape of Nothingness. It is called dim and elusive. Face it, yet you do not see its head. Follow it, yet you do not see its back (14). Look at it, and there is not enough to see. Listen to it, and there is not enough to hear (35). The bright Way seems to be obscure, the Way forward seems to be backwards, and the smooth Way seems to be rough (41). Invisible. Nevertheless, it seems to exist. I do not know whose child it is, but it seems to predate the Emperor (4). It seems to exist forever and using it is no hard work (6).

Do not leave home in order to learn about the world. Do not look through the window in order to learn about the Way of nature. The more that people travel far away the less they know. Therefore, sages do not travel and yet they know. They do not see and yet they name. They do not act and yet they achieve (47).

In speaking, the goodness is truth (8). True words seem to be paradoxical (78). True words are not pleasing. Pleasing words are not true (81). Plain truth seems to change; the greatest square is without edges; the greatest talent matures late; the greatest sound is a rare tone; and the greatest form is without shape (41). The greatest achievement seems to be incomplete. Yet, its usefulness is not reduced. The greatest fullness seems to be empty. Yet, its usefulness is never exhausted. The greatest straightness seems to bend. The greatest skill seems clumsy. The greatest triumph seems insufficient (45).

If everyone in the world recognises beauty as beautiful, then there is already ugliness. If everyone recognizes good as goodness, then there is already badness. Therefore, Existence and Non-existence generate each other. Difficult and easy turn into each other. Long and short shape each other. High and low fill each other. Tone and voice harmonise each other. Before and after follow each other forever (2). The five colours will blind people's eyes. The five tones will deafen people's ears. The five flavours will refresh people's mouth. Galloping and hunting in the field will overexcite people's minds. Goods that are difficult to obtain will harm people (12).

PROJECTION

Projection—part of interaction that refers to managing the outgoing information flow from the mind towards the sensory reality. The exhaustive options provided by projection for maximizing success are to *Reveal and Conceal* information (Schade, Glossary Nemonik Thinking, 2016).

Lao Zi

Those who stand on tiptoe do not stand firm. Those who display themselves are without brilliance. Those who regard themselves are without honour. Those who boast about themselves are without merit. Those who are arrogant are without development. Their Way is called: *"Leftover food and unnecessary action."* These things are disgusting. Therefore, those who have desires will not succeed (24).

Bend then be preserved. Twist then be straightened. Empty then be filled. Exhaust then be renewed. Lack then receive. Have surplus then be confused. Therefore, sages hold on to the One. Accordingly, they are the shepherds of the world. They do not display themselves. Therefore, they are brilliant. They do not regard themselves. Therefore, they are honoured. They do not boast about themselves. Therefore, they have merit. They are not arrogant.

Therefore, they will develop. They do not strive. Therefore, no one can strive with them (22).

Teachers of humanity discus and teach people that violent people will achieve nothing but death. I will use that as the father of my teachings (42).

NEMONIKS

MENTAL NEMONIKS

OBJECTIVE-1

Objective mindmode—way of rational thinking that deals with the natural order of the sensory reality, which can be described by natural laws and facts that make nature predictable. Objective refers to a description of reality that is independent of what anyone believes. The objective mindmode is a conscious way of thinking that is activated by concentration. In contrast to the collective mindmode, the objective mindmode pertains to the laws of nature. In contrast to the creative mindmode, the objective mindmode will increase our knowledge step-by-step in an incremental way. The objective mindmode uses the mental order of reason to deal with the natural order of reality. Objective thinking generates science. Sir Isaac Newton was the one of the first scientists to describe objectively the laws of the sensory reality. Albert Einstein and Max Planck extended Newton's ideas into the extrasensory reality. Objective specialists are found where proficiency in natural laws is crucial such as in science and technology (Schade, Glossary Nemonik Thinking, 2016).

Lao Zi

Study and eliminate mysteries. Inspect them competently without flaws (10). Adhere to the present Way in order to manage the present Existence. Use it to understand its ancient origin. That is called the principle of the Way (14).

COLLECTIVE-2

Collective mindmode—way of rational thinking that generates artificial rules, which determine the rights and obligations of individuals within a collective and makes their behaviours predictable. Collective refers to an organized group of people with a common goal such as a family, business, tribe, nation, or the entire human race. Artificial refers to that part of the sensory reality that is manmade. The collective mindmode uses the mental order of reason to deal with the artificial order of the sensory reality. The Chinese philosopher Confucius was an important advocate of collective thinking. Collective specialists are found where proficiency in artificial rules is crucial such as in accountancy, bureaucracy, court, and government (Schade, Glossary Nemonik Thinking, 2016).

Lao Zi

If the world possesses the Way, then race horses will be kept for their manure. If the world is without the Way, then war horses will be bred in the suburbs (46). If the great Way is rejected, then there will be benevolence and justice. Knowledge and cleverness will appear and then there is great hypocrisy. Family relationships will be disharmonious and then there is animal dirt everywhere. The State's household will be a confused disorder and then there is bureaucracy (18).

Superior benevolence acts and yet there is no use in those actions. Superior justice acts and there is purpose in those actions. Superior propriety acts and if there is no agreement, then the arms are bared. Therefore, after the Way is lost there will be virtue. After virtue is lost, there will be benevolence. After benevolence is lost, there will be justice. After justice is lost, there will be propriety. Those who have propriety possess only a thin layer of loyalty and sincerity, which is the beginning of disorder (38).

People are born soft and weak. They die, hard and strong. All-things, grasses, and trees are born soft and fragile. They die, dry and brittle. Therefore, the hard and strong are called companions of death. The soft and weak are the companions of life. Hence, a strong army will not win. A strong tree will be broken. Therefore, the strong and big occupy the low positions. The soft and weak occupy the high positions (76).

The Great Road is very smooth. Yet, people prefer the narrow winding roads. Their palaces are very clean. Their fields are overgrown with weeds. Their storehouses are very empty (53). People are hungry, because their food taxes are high. Therefore, they are hungry. Common people cannot be governed, because their leaders act for their own purposes. Therefore, the people cannot be governed. People take death lightly, because they seek to live substantially. Therefore, they take death lightly. Only those who do not act for the purpose of living are knowledgeable at valuing life (75).

Use the Way to assist the leaders of people (30). Sages have a saying that states: *"Accept the country's shame and be called the Kingdom's leader. Accept the country's misfortune and be called the world's King."* True words seem to be paradoxical (78). How are the river and the sea able to be the Kings of a hundred valleys? They use competently their low position. Therefore, they are able to be Kings of a hundred valleys. Therefore, sages who desire to be above the people must place themselves below them. Those who desire to lead people must place themselves behind them. Therefore, they stay above and the people will not weight them down. They stay in front and the people will not harm them. Everyone in the world will be happy to elect them without objection. Having no purpose, they do not strive. Therefore the world cannot strive with them (66). Those of value speak about their plans and succeed in completing their affairs. Yet, the common people will say; it happened naturally (17).

Competent leaders will take a low position. That is called the virtue of not striving. That is called employing people. That is called matching with nature. It is the ultimate principle of the Ancients (68). Carry the 'corps de esprit' and unite it inseparable with the One. Concentrate vital energy and be as soft as an infant (10). Love the people and rule the country without using knowledge (10). Great leaders are those known by their subjects to exist. Next are those that are loved and praised. Next are those that are feared. Next are those low ones who are insulting. If there is not enough trust, then there is distrust (17). Those who wear embroidered coloured silk, carry sharp swords, gorge on food, and have a surplus of goods and resources, are called 'boasting thieves'. Boasting thieves are not the Way (53).

If Marquises and Kings do not use superior nobility, then fear that they will be overthrown. Therefore, the noble must use the ignoble as their foundation. The high must use the low as their foundation. Therefore, Marquises and Kings call themselves unkindly 'orphans and widowers'. They use that ignobility incorrectly as their foundation. Therefore, they give too much honour without honour (39). People dislike being unrelated orphans and widowers. Yet, Kings and Marquises use those names for themselves (42).

Use justice when ruling the State. Use surprise when employing armies. Use no effort when taking the world.

How do I know it is like this? Only after this. The more prohibitions there are in the world, the poorer the people will be. The more sharp weapons people have, the more the State's household will be confused. The more people know, the stranger the things they begin to develop. Rules increase the content of the law and, therefore, there will be more criminals. Hence, the saying of the sages states: *"I practice Non-action and the people will transform themselves. I am tranquil and the people will perfect themselves. I use no effort and the people will become wealthy by themselves. I desire not to desire and the people will become simple by themselves"* (57). Sages will not divide great organisations (28). If an organisation is established titles will appear. If titles appear, then know that it is time to stop. Know when to stop and there will be no danger (32).

The Ancients said: *"Do not use the Way to enlighten people."* Instead, use it to keep them simple. People are difficult to rule if they use their knowledge. Therefore, using knowledge to rule the country is betraying the country. Using no knowledge to rule the country is benefiting the country. Remember always those two things. Examine also the principle. Always remembering to examine the principle is called profound virtue. Profound virtue is deep. Even far away things return to it. The great order is perfect (65).

Use justice when ruling the State. Use surprise when employing armies. Use no effort when taking the world (57).

If one wants to take the world, then one should always use no effort. When effort is needed, then there is never enough to take the world (48). Ruling a large country is like enjoying small delicacies. Use the Way to attend to the world, then spirits will have no power (60). Activity overcomes the cold. Tranquillity overcomes the heat. Hence, pure tranquillity can be used to regulate the world (45).

Discard adoration and reject knowledge and the people will benefit a hundred times. Discard benevolence and reject righteousness and the people will return to filial piety and compassion. Discard cleverness and reject profit and there will be no burglars and thieves. These three declarations could be regarded to be inadequate slogans. Therefore, let the people have also institutions. Show modesty and embrace simplicity. Lack selfishness and restrain desires (19).

Do not promote the knowledgeable and the people will not strive. Do not admire goods that are difficult to obtain and the people will not steal. Do not display what is desirable and the people will not revolt. Therefore, sages rule by emptying the minds of people, filling their stomachs, weakening their ambitions, and strengthening their bones. Let the people be always without knowledge and without desire. Let those who know, not dare to act but stop. Act with Non-action, then there will be no anarchy (3). The five colours will blind people's eyes. The five tones will deafen people's ears. The five flavours will refresh people's mouth. Galloping and hunting in the field will overexcite people's minds. Goods that are difficult to obtain will harm people. Therefore, sages will rule for the stomach and not for the eyes. Therefore, reject that and accept this (12).

In ruling people and working with nature there is nothing like frugality. Only those who are frugal are called to early service. Prepare for the call to serve early by a significant accumulation of virtue. If there is a significant accumulation of virtue, then nothing is impossible. If nothing is impossible, then one's limits are unknown. If one's limits are unknown, then one may possess the country. Possess the Mother of the country and accordingly endure long. That is called: having deep roots and a strong foundation. Having a long life through a lasting regard for the Way (59).

A large country should take a low position. It is the intersection of the world. It is the female of the world. The female always uses tranquillity to overcome the male. She is tranquil. Therefore, she is better in a low position. Hence, a large country should use a lower position than a small country, when associating with that smaller country. A small country should use a lower position than a large country, when associating with that larger country. Therefore, some might take the lower position to associate. Others might be in the lower position to associate. Those in a large country only desire to merge and raise people. Those in a small country only desire to join other business people. They all obtain what they desire. Therefore, the larger one better acts as the lowest one (61).

In a small country with a few people, let everybody have many tools, but not use them. Let the people be serious about death and not move far away. Let them have carriages without using them. Let them have weapons without displaying them. Let them return to knotted cords and use them. Sweeten their food and beautify their clothes. Enjoy their customs and secure their dwellings. Neighbouring countries will see each other in the distance. They hear each other's chickens and dogs. Nevertheless, the people die of old age and have never visited each other (80).

Let the people have institutions. Show modesty and embrace simplicity. Lack selfishness and restrain desires (19). Flattery and rebuke: how much do they differ from each other? Satisfaction and dissatisfaction: how much do they differ from each other (20)? Favour and disgrace are just like distress. They cause great suffering just like the body. Why saying that favour and disgrace are just like distress? Favour is inferior. Receiving it is like distress and losing it is like distress. Whether it is called favour or disgrace, it is like distress. Why saying that it cost great suffering just like the body? Why do I have great suffering? That is, because I have a body. If I had no body, how could I suffer? Therefore, those who purposely value their body for serving the world can be entrusted with the purpose of the world. Those who purposely love their body for the world can be entrusted with the world (13).

What everybody fears, one has to fear as well. Everybody stares at me. They do not stop. Everybody is very happy. Just like a big sacrificial feast in the village and stepping on stage in the springtime. I am quiet and not predictable. Just like a baby that has not coughed yet. Tired; without a place to return to. Everybody has a surplus. Yet, only I seem to be lacking. I am a very stupid fool in other people's minds. Everybody is very clear. Only I seem to be confused. Everybody is very certain. Only I seem to be very uncertain. They are indifferent. It is like staring at the sea. It is like having no place to rest. Everybody has a purpose. Only I am stubborn and my purpose seems to be ridiculous. Only I desire to differ from other people and value the food from the Mother (20).

Attack with sharp weapons to become victorious, but use them without satisfaction. Those who are satisfied by it, like to kill people. Those who like to kill people cannot achieve the goals of the State (31). Armies are the tools of misfortune. They are disgusting. Therefore, those who possess the Way will not claim them (31). Do not use soldiers to force the world. Such actions are likely to rebound. Where armies have camped only thorny bushes will grow. Those who are competent succeed and stop in time. Do not dare to take power. Succeed without boasting. Succeed without attacking. Succeed without arrogance. Succeed without excess. That is called succeeding without force (30). The soft and weak will overcome the strong. A fish should not leave the deep water. The sharp weapons of the State should not be used in view of the people (36).

Rules increase the content of the law and, therefore, there will be more criminals (57). The more prohibitions there are in the world, the poorer the people will be (57). If the laws are very lax, then the people will have extreme surpluses. If the laws are very strict, then the people will have extreme shortages and misfortune. Misfortune is fortune's place to hide. Fortune is misfortune's place to hide (58). When people do not fear authority, then greater authority will appear. Do not take their dwellings by force. Do not reject them a place to live. Only, if they are not rejected, then they will not reject you. Therefore, sages know themselves, but do not display themselves. They love themselves, but do not admire themselves. Therefore, reject that and accept this (72).

If people never fear death, how could the use of executions scare them? If people always fear death and act abnormal, how could I dare to seize, hold, and execute them? If people always fear certain death, then there is always someone in charge of executing them. Those who act on behalf of the one that is in charge of the executions, execute as if they act on behalf of the Master Carpenter. From those who act on behalf of the Master Carpenter only a few will not cut their hands (74). The teachers of humanity discus and teach people that violent people will achieve nothing but death. I will use that as the father of my teachings (42).

CREATIVE-3

Creative mindmode—way of affectorial thinking that deals with the unknown or inexperienced aspects of reality by generating creative affecters. Creative affecters include discoveries, fantasies, ideas, innovations, insights, inspirations, inventions, novelties, etc. The seventeen nemoniks are memory prompts and markers for mind mapping that foster the associative processes of the creative mindmode. The creative mindmode uses mental disorganisation or chaos to deal with the chaos of . For example, brainstorming is a random process that fosters creativity. The creative mindmode provides new experiences and, therefore, it moves people outside their comfort zone. Joy Paul Guilford and Edward de Bono extended our knowledge about creative thinking. Guilford introduced *'divergent thinking'* and de Bono *'lateral thinking'*. Creative specialists are found where originality is crucial such as in art, design, invention, research, etc. (Schade, Glossary Nemonik Thinking, 2016).

Lao Zi

No comments.

REACTIVE-4

Reactive mindmode—way of affectorial thinking that deals with the chaos of reality by habituating mindsets that generate reactive affecters. Reactive affecters include beliefs, common sense, desires, emotions, habits, heuristics, impulses, informal logic, intuitions, reactions, reflexes, routines, sensibility, skills, etc. The reactive mindmode uses mental preparation or order to deal with the chaos of reality. It is the aim of the reactive mindmode to optimize your mental and physical perfection. However, the reactive mindmode is a product of the past. It relies on your experience and, therefore, it keeps you within your comfort zone. The Chinese philosopher Lao Zi advocated reactive thinking. Reactive specialists are found where individual perfection is crucial such as in chess, driving, martial arts, sports, surgery, etc. (Schade, Glossary Nemonik Thinking, 2016).

Lao Zi

I have always three treasures that I keep and protect. The first one is called compassion. The second one is called frugality. The third one is called humbleness (67).

Those who are compassionate can be courageous (67). Those who abandon compassion and are yet courageous, they will certainly die. Those who use compassion to attack will triumph. Those who use it to defend will stand firm. Nature will protect them with a wall of compassion (67. Discard benevolence and reject righteousness and the people will return to filial piety and compassion (19).

Those who are frugal can be generous (67). Those who abandon their frugality and are yet generous, they will certainly die (67).

In ruling people and working with nature there is nothing like frugality. Only those who are frugal are called to early service. Prepare for the call to serve early by a significant accumulation of virtue. If there is a significant accumulation of virtue, then nothing is impossible. If nothing is impossible, then one's limits are unknown. If one's limits are unknown, then one may possess the country. Possess the Mother of the country and accordingly endure long. That is called: having deep roots and a strong foundation. Having a long life through a lasting regard for the Way (59). Sages save people always competently by not rejecting them. Not rejected things are resources. Accordingly, that is called brilliant (27).

Show modesty and embrace simplicity. Lack selfishness and restrain desires (19). The Way is forever nameless. If Marquises and Kings could follow it, then All-things would transform themselves. If this transformation would cause desire, then I would suppress it by using the simplicity of the nameless. Suppressing it by using the simplicity of the nameless will not disgrace them. Use tranquillity without disgrace and the world will regulate itself (37).

Those who do not dare to act as the first of the world can be successful leaders of affairs (67). Those who abandon their humbleness and are yet leading; they will certainly die (67). Admiring wealth and arrogance brings personal loss and misfortune (9). Those who stand on tiptoe do not stand firm. Those who display themselves are without brilliance. Those who regard themselves are without honour. Those who boast about themselves are without merit. Those who are arrogant are without development. Their Way is called: *"Leftover food and unnecessary action."* These things are disgusting. Therefore, those who have desires will not succeed (24). Their palaces are very clean. Their fields are overgrown with weeds. Their storehouses are very empty. Those who wear embroidered coloured silk, carry sharp swords, gorge on food, and have a surplus of goods and resources, are called 'boasting thieves'. Boasting thieves are not the Way (53).

The ones called the 'Ancients' said: *"Those who bend will be preserved."* Is that saying insignificant? However, true preservation was their return (22). Those who are competent succeed and stop in time. Do not dare to take power. Succeed without boasting. Succeed without attacking. Succeed without arrogance. Succeed without excess. That is called succeeding without force (30). Sages know themselves, but do not display themselves (71). They do not display themselves. Therefore, they are brilliant. They do not regard themselves. Therefore, they are honoured. They do not boast about themselves. Therefore, they have merit. They are not arrogant. Therefore, they will develop (22). Sages are interfering but not cutting, sharp but not stabbing, straight but not rigid, and bright but not dazzling (58).

Tranquillity is the sovereign of rashness (26). The female always uses tranquillity to overcome the male. She is tranquil (61). Use tranquillity without disgrace and the world will regulate itself (37). Tranquillity overcomes the heat. Hence, pure tranquillity can be used to regulate the world (45). Misfortune is fortune's place to hide. Fortune is misfortune's place to hide. Who knows their extremes? There is no normal. Normal turns around and becomes abnormal. Good turns around and becomes evil. That has confused everybody for a long time (58). Concentrate on removing extremes. Nurse tranquillity faithfully. All-things around us rise, and I watch them return. Those things are numerous and each one returns to its roots. Returning to the roots is called tranquillity. Tranquillity is called returning to order. Returning to order is a constant. Knowing this constant is brilliant. Not acknowledging this constant is arrogant. Arrogance causes misfortune. Knowing this constant is embracing. Embracing is honourable. Honourable is Kingly. Kingly is natural. Natural is the Way. The Way is forever. It provides a content life without danger (16).

Concentrate vital energy and be as soft as an infant (10). Be the valley of the world and the eternal virtue will always be enough. If the eternal virtue is always enough, then you will return to simplicity (28). To perceive the small is called brilliant. Following the soft is called strength. Use its light to join its brilliance again. Not losing life to disaster is called following the constant (52). The softest will overcome the hardest. The weakest will overcome the strongest. Nobody in the world does not know this. Yet, nobody does practise it (78).

OPERATIONAL NEMONIKS

ADVANCE-5

Advance—spatial nemonik that prompts the mind to decrease the distance to the goal (Schade, Glossary Nemonik Thinking, 2016).

Lao Zi

Succeed without attacking (30). Warriors have a saying that states: *"I do not dare to act as a host, but act as a guest. I do not dare to advance an inch, but retreat a foot."* That is called: moving without moving. Rolling up the sleeves without showing an arm. Be without resistance. Hold without weapons. No greater misfortune than meeting no resistance. Meeting no resistance is close to losing my treasures. Therefore, when equal armies face each other the reluctant one will win (69). Competent warriors do not like war. Competent chiefs will not get angry. Competent conquerors will not engage. Competent leaders will take a low position. That is called the virtue of not striving. That is called employing people. That is called matching with nature. It is the ultimate principle of the Ancients (68).

STAY-6

Stay—spatial nemonik that prompts the mind to maintain the same distance to the goal (Schade, Glossary Nemonik Thinking, 2016).

Lao Zi

No comments.

RETREAT-7

Retreat—spatial nemonik that prompts the mind to increase the distance to the goal (Schade, Glossary Nemonik Thinking, 2016).

Lao Zi

When merit is achieved, withdrawing yourself is the Way of nature (9). Accordingly, sages withdraw themselves. Yet they are first. They put themselves outside. Yet they are inside. Because they are selfless, therefore, their self-interest is fulfilled (7). Concentrate on removing extremes. Nurse tranquillity faithfully (16). Be without resistance. Hold without weapons. No greater misfortune than meeting no resistance. Meeting no resistance is close to losing my treasures. Therefore, when equal armies face each other the reluctant one will win (69).

ACCUMULATE-8

Accumulate—material nemonik that prompts the mind to increase the amount of matter that is under control (Schade, Glossary Nemonik Thinking, 2016).

Lao Zi

Accumulating and filling up is not as good as stopping in time. Hammer it too sharp and it cannot last long. A room filled with gold and jade cannot be defended competently (9). Admiring wealth and arrogance brings personal loss and misfortune (9). No greater suffering than having extreme desires. No greater misfortune than not knowing what is enough. No misfortune is more disastrous than the desire to accumulate. Therefore, know that enough is enough and there will be always enough (46). Those who have desires will not succeed (24). Those who know what is enough are rich (33). Those who are competent have not much. Those who have much are not competent (81). Have surplus then be confused (22).

Sages desire not to desire and do not admire goods that are difficult to obtain (64). Sages do not hoard. Since they are used to act for other people, they receive more possessions for themselves. Since they are used to give to other people, they have much more themselves (81). Sages reject extremes, reject grandeur, and reject extravagance (29). Those who keep the Way do not desire fullness. Only those who desire no fullness are therefore able to exhaust themselves without renewal (15). Those who are competent succeed and stop in time. Do not dare to take power (30). Do not desire the great splendour of jade, but the grace of natural rock (39). Generate All-things and raise them. Generate but do not possess. Develop but do not exploit. This is called profound virtue (10).

Be always without desire and see the details. Have always desires and see the limits. These two things occur together. Different names with the same meaning. Profoundly mysterious, they are the gateway to many details (1). If anyone would desire to take the world and interfere with it, I see that they have no alternative. The world is a container of energy that cannot be interfered with. Those who interfere will fail. Those who hold will lose (29). Fame or life? What is closer? Life or wealth? What is worth more? Gain or loss? What hurts more? Most people love to spend a lot. The larger their hoard the more they have to lose. Therefore, know what is enough and there will be no disgrace. Know when to stop and there will be no danger. Accordingly, one will endure long (44).

PRESERVE-9

Preserve—material nemonik that prompts the mind to maintain the same amount of matter that is under control (Schade, Glossary Nemonik Thinking, 2016).

Lao Zi

Those who are courageous in daring will be killed. Those who are courageous in not daring will live (73). Emerging into life is entering into death. Three in ten are companions of life. Three in ten are companions of death. Three in ten people live extremely and move into the realm of death. What is the reason? That is because they live extremely. They are incompetent in hiding, listening, and conserving their lives. Do not walk through the hills in order to meet rhinoceroses and tigers. Do not join the army in order to carry weapons. Rhinoceroses have no place to ram their horns. Tigers have no place to strike their claws. Soldiers have no place to thrust their swords. What is the reason? Because sages avoid the realm of death (50).

In ruling people and working with nature there is nothing like frugality. Only those who are frugal are called to early service (59). Sages save people always competently by not rejecting them. Not rejected things are resources. Accordingly, that is called brilliant. Therefore, competent people are the teachers of incompetent people. Incompetent people are the resources of competent people. Those who do not value their teachers, or do not love their resources, although knowledgeable, are greatly confused. This is called the essential detail (27).

DISPOSE-10

Dispose—material nemonik that prompts the mind to decrease the amount matter that is under control (Schade, Glossary Nemonik Thinking, 2016).

Lao Zi

In giving, the goodness is benevolence (8). Concentrate on removing extremes (16). It is the Way of Nature to take from what is plenty and give to what is not enough. However, the Way of People is different. They take from what is not enough and give to what is plenty. Hence, those who have plenty and give to those in the world who have not enough are the only ones who possess the Way (77). Since sages are used to give to other people, they have much more themselves (81). Empty then be filled. Exhaust then be renewed. Lack then receive (22). Use the Way and it cannot be depleted (35). Look at it, and there is not enough to see. Listen to it, and there is not enough to hear. However, use it and it cannot be depleted (35).

The Way of Nature is beneficial and without harm. Accordingly, the Way of People should be action without strive (81). The Way of nature is not to strive, but to overcome through competence (73). Having no purpose, sages do not strive. Therefore the world cannot strive with them (66). Sages do not strive. Therefore, no one can strive with them (22). Superior goodness is like water. The goodness of water benefits All-things and it does not strive. It occupies places everybody dislikes. Therefore, it is close to the Way (8). Only those who do not strive will therefore not fail (8). Competent warriors do not like war. Competent chiefs will not get angry. Competent conquerors will not engage. Competent leaders will take a low position. That is called the virtue of not striving. That is called employing people. That is called matching with nature. It is the ultimate principle of the Ancients (68).

Calm a great hate and certainly some hate will remain. How could this be considered competent? Therefore, sages adhere to orthodox agreements and do not obligate other people by purpose. Therefore, those with virtue will uphold the agreement. Those without virtue will uphold the details. The Way of Nature has no favourites. It is always with the competent people (79). Only those who do not act for the purpose of living are knowledgeable at valuing life (75).

ACT-11

Act—temporal nemonik that prompts the mind to change or move matter in space and time (Schade, Glossary Nemonik Thinking, 2016).

Lao Zi

Let me have pure knowledge. When walking on the Great Road, the only thing I fear is action (53. Those who daily pursue knowledge will expand. Those who daily pursue the Way will contract. Contract and contract until there is Non-action left. There is Non-action and yet there is action. If one wants to take the world, then one should always use no effort. When effort is needed, then there is never enough to take the world (48). If anyone would desire to take the world and interfere with it, I see that they have no alternative. The world is a container of energy that cannot be interfered with. Those who interfere will fail. Those who hold will lose (29). Those who act will fail. Those who hold will lose (64).

Sages manage their affairs with Non-action. They carry out their teachings without speaking. All-things rise, but do not initiate them. Act, but do not rely on it. Succeed, but do not claim. Only that what is not claimed can therefore not be taken away (2). Sages act, but do not rely on it. They succeed, but do not claim (77). Sages will use Non-action.

Therefore, they will not fail. They will not hold. Therefore, they will not lose (64). Sages can achieve greatness, because they do not act great. Therefore, they can achieve greatness (34). They do not act and yet they achieve (47). Act with Non-action. Work without effort. Taste without savouring (63). Generate but do not possess. Act but do not rely on it. Grow but do not exploit. This is called profound virtue (51). Only those who do not act for the purpose of living are knowledgeable at valuing life (75). Since sages are used to act for other people, they receive more possessions for themselves (81).

Those who act on behalf of the one that is in charge of the executions, execute as if they act on behalf of the Master Carpenter. From those who act on behalf of the Master Carpenter only a few will not cut their hands (74). Heaviness is the foundation of lightness. Tranquillity is the sovereign of rashness. Therefore, great men who travel all day will not leave their heavy wagons. Although, there is a walled guest house in a quiet place nearby, they remain aloof. Just like a lord with ten thousand chariots who considers himself less important than the State. Lightness will lose the foundation. Rashness will lose the sovereign (26).

The softest of the world will overcome the hardest of the world. What is without substance will penetrate what is without gaps. Therefore, I know that there is benefit in Non-action. Teaching without speaking and Non-action will benefit the whole world. Only a few competent people can attain this (43). Those who are courageous in daring will be killed. Those who are courageous in not daring will live (73).

WAIT-12

Wait—temporal nemonik that prompts the mind to delay an action until it is the right time for that action (Schade, Glossary Nemonik Thinking, 2016).

Lao Zi

In action, the goodness is timing (8). Those who are competent succeed and stop in time (30). If an organisation is established titles will appear. If titles appear, then know that it is time to stop. Know when to stop and there will be no danger (32. Know when to stop and there will be no danger. Accordingly, one will endure long (44). Accumulating and filling up is not as good as stopping in time (9). Do not stir mud and it will slowly clear (15).

PREPARE-13

Prepare—temporal nemonik that prompts the mind to get ready for action. Preparation includes analysing, decision-making, learning, mind management, negotiating, organizing, planning, positioning, prioritizing, risk-management, fostering leadership, setting goals, internalizing nemonik thinking, time management, training, etc. Preparation is productive if it is based on proactivity, while it is counterproductive if it is used as an excuse for procrastination. The 80/20 rule supports the notion that perfect preparation is counterproductive. Even imperfect things and actions might be extremely useful (Schade, Glossary Nemonik Thinking, 2016).

Lao Zi

Why did the Ancients value the protection of the Way? Did they not say: *"Use it to obtain what you seek and use it to escape what you suffer."* Therefore, it is valuable for the whole world (62). The Way is simple and plans with competence. The net of nature is very extensive. It dredges and nothing escapes (73). Those of value speak about their plans and succeed in completing their affairs. Yet, the common people will say; it happened naturally (17).

Misfortune is fortune's place to hide. Fortune is misfortune's place to hide (58). Fame or life? What is closer? Life or wealth? What is worth more? Gain or loss? What hurts more (44)? In dwelling, the goodness is location. In thinking, the goodness is depth. In giving, the goodness is benevolence. In speaking, the goodness is truth. In ruling, the goodness is order. In working, the goodness is skill. In action, the goodness is timing (8). File the sharpness of All-things. Untangle their disorder. Soften their glare. Merge their dust. This is called profound unification. It cannot be achieved by attachment. Neither can it be achieved by detachment. It cannot be achieved by benefit. Neither can it be achieved by harm. It cannot be achieved by admiration. Also, it cannot be achieved by contempt. Therefore, the world admires it (56).

Having no purpose, sages do not strive. Therefore the world cannot strive with them (66). They do not strive. Therefore, no one can strive with them (22). Sages reject extremes, reject grandeur, and reject extravagance (29). Concentrate on removing extremes. Nurse tranquillity faithfully (16). Returning to the roots is called tranquillity. Tranquillity is called returning to order. Returning to order is a constant. Knowing this constant is brilliant. Not acknowledging this constant is arrogant. Arrogance causes misfortune. Knowing this constant is embracing (16).

Act with Non-action. Work without effort. Taste without savouring. Make the large small and the many few. Repay hatred with kindness. Pursue the difficult, while it is easy. Act large, while it is still small. The world's most difficult things arise from the most easy ones. The world's largest things arise from the smallest ones. Therefore, all sages will avoid great actions. Hence, they can achieve greatness. Those who make rash promises are certainly difficult to trust.

Those who regard everything as easy will have certainly many difficulties. Therefore, sages regard everything as difficult. Hence, they have no difficulties in the end (63).

To fold something, it must have been unfolded before. To weaken something, it must have been strengthened before. To abandon something, it must have been attached before. To seize something, it must have been separated before. This is called profound brilliance (36). That what is at rest is easy to hold. That what is not manifest is easy to plan. That what is fragile is easy to break. That what is small is easy to scatter. Act when it has not happened yet. Control it when it is not chaotic yet. A tree that takes both arms to embrace grows from a little cutting. Nine-tenth of a tower rises from a simple basket of earth. A thousand meters height starts from under your feet. Those who act will fail. Those who hold will lose. Therefore, sages will use Non-action. Therefore, they will not fail. They will not hold. Therefore, they will not lose. In handling their affairs, people fail often close to their success. Therefore, be as careful at the end as at the beginning. Then affairs will not fail. Therefore, sages desire not to desire and do not admire goods that are difficult to obtain. They learn not to learn and repair the mistakes of others. Sages complement the nature of all All-things, but they do not dare to act (64).

ACCEPT-14

Accept—perceptual nemonik that prompts the mind to accept the incoming information as a true description of the sensory reality. One can adopt a strict or lax decision criterion (Schade, Glossary Nemonik Thinking, 2016).

Lao Zi

Sages have a saying that states: *"Accept the country's shame and be called the Kingdom's leader. Accept the country's misfortune and be called the world's King."* True words seem to be paradoxical (78). Sages save people always competently by not rejecting them. Not rejected things are resources. Accordingly, that is called brilliant (27).

REJECT-15

Reject—perceptual nemonik that prompts the mind to refuse the incoming information as a true description of the sensory reality (Schade, Glossary Nemonik Thinking, 2016).

Lao Zi

Those who pretend to know the future are the fruitless flowers of the Way and the chiefs of fools. Therefore, great men occupy the thick and do not occupy the thin. Occupy the fruit, but do not occupy the fruitless flowers. Therefore, reject that and accept this (38).

True words are not pleasing. Pleasing words are not true. Those who know are not educated. Those who are educated do not know (81). Those who speak do not know. Block the exchange and close the doors (56). Block the exchange and close the doors; and to the end of life there will be no hard work. Open the exchange and meddle in affairs; and to the end of life there will be no safety (52).

Discard knowledge and there are no worries (20). Discard adoration and reject knowledge and the people will benefit a hundred times. Discard benevolence and reject righteousness and the people will return to filial piety and compassion. Discard cleverness and reject profit and there will be no burglars and thieves (19). Things may succeed or may fail. They may be hot or may be cold. They may be strong or may be weak. They may grow or may decay. Therefore, sages reject extremes, reject grandeur, and reject extravagance (29).

If the great Way is rejected, then there will be benevolence and justice. Knowledge and cleverness will appear and then there is great hypocrisy. Family relationships will be disharmonious and then there is animal dirt everywhere. The State's household will be a confused disorder and then there is bureaucracy (18). Do not reject others a place to live. Only, if they are not rejected, then they will not reject you (72).

REVEAL-16

Reveal—projectional nemonik that prompts the mind to project true information to the sensory reality (Schade, Glossary Nemonik Thinking, 2016).

Lao Zi

In speaking, the goodness is truth (8). Sages have a saying that states: *"Accept the country's shame and be called the Kingdom's leader. Accept the country's misfortune and be called the world's King."* True words seem to be paradoxical (78). I have always three treasures that I keep and protect. The first one is called compassion. The second one is called frugality. The third one is called humbleness (67).

Bend then be preserved. Twist then be straightened. Empty then be filled. Exhaust then be renewed. Lack then receive. Have surplus then be confused. Therefore, sages hold on to the One. Accordingly, they are the shepherds of the world. They do not display themselves. Therefore, they are brilliant. They do not regard themselves. Therefore, they are honoured. They do not boast about themselves. Therefore, they have merit. They are not arrogant. Therefore, they will develop. They do not strive. Therefore, no one can strive with them. The ones called the 'Ancients' said: *"Those who bend will be preserved."* Is that saying insignificant? However, true preservation was their return (22).

Sages who desire to be above the people must place themselves below them. Those who desire to lead people must place themselves behind them. Therefore, they stay above and the people will not weight them down. They stay in front and the people will not harm them (66).

CONCEAL-17

Conceal—projectional nemonik that prompts the mind to project false information to the sensory reality (Schade, Glossary Nemonik Thinking, 2016).

Lao Zi

Those who stand on tiptoe do not stand firm. Those who display themselves are without brilliance. Those who regard themselves are without honour. Those who boast about themselves are without merit. Those who are arrogant are without development. Their Way is called: *"Leftover food and unnecessary action."* These things are disgusting (24). Those who wear embroidered coloured silk, carry sharp swords, gorge on food, and have a surplus of goods and resources, are called 'boasting thieves'. Boasting thieves are not the Way (53).

Speaking seldom is natural (23). Those who know do not speak. Those who speak do not know (56). Sages manage their affairs with Non-action. They carry out their teachings without speaking (2). Teaching without speaking and Non-action will benefit the whole world. Only a few competent people can attain this (43).

Sages do not desire to display their knowledge (77). The Ancients said: *"Do not use the Way to enlighten people."* Instead, use it to keep them simple. People are difficult to rule if they use their knowledge. Therefore, using knowledge to rule the country is betraying the country. Using no knowledge to rule the country is benefiting the country (65). Let the people be always without knowledge and without desire (3). Let the people have weapons without displaying them (81). A fish should not leave the deep water. The sharp weapons of the State should not be used in view of the people (36).

Sages know themselves, but do not display themselves. They love themselves, but do not admire themselves (72). Sages do not display themselves. Therefore, they are brilliant. They do not regard themselves. Therefore, they are honoured. They do not boast about themselves. Therefore, they have merit. They are not arrogant. Therefore, they will develop. They do not strive. Therefore, no one can strive with them (22). Discard adoration and reject knowledge and the people will benefit a hundred times (19). Show modesty and embrace simplicity. Lack selfishness and restrain desires (19).

Great leaders are those known by their subjects to exist. Next are those that are loved and praised. Next are those that are feared. Next are those low ones who are insulting (17). Those of value speak about their plans and succeed in completing their affairs. Yet, the common people will say; it happened naturally (17).

My words are very easy to understand and very easy to apply. Yet, people cannot understand them and they cannot apply them. My words have precedence and my affairs have a sovereign, but they do not understand that. Therefore, they do not understand me. I am valuable to those few who understand me. Therefore, sages wear cheap cloth and conceal jade (70).

RESULTS

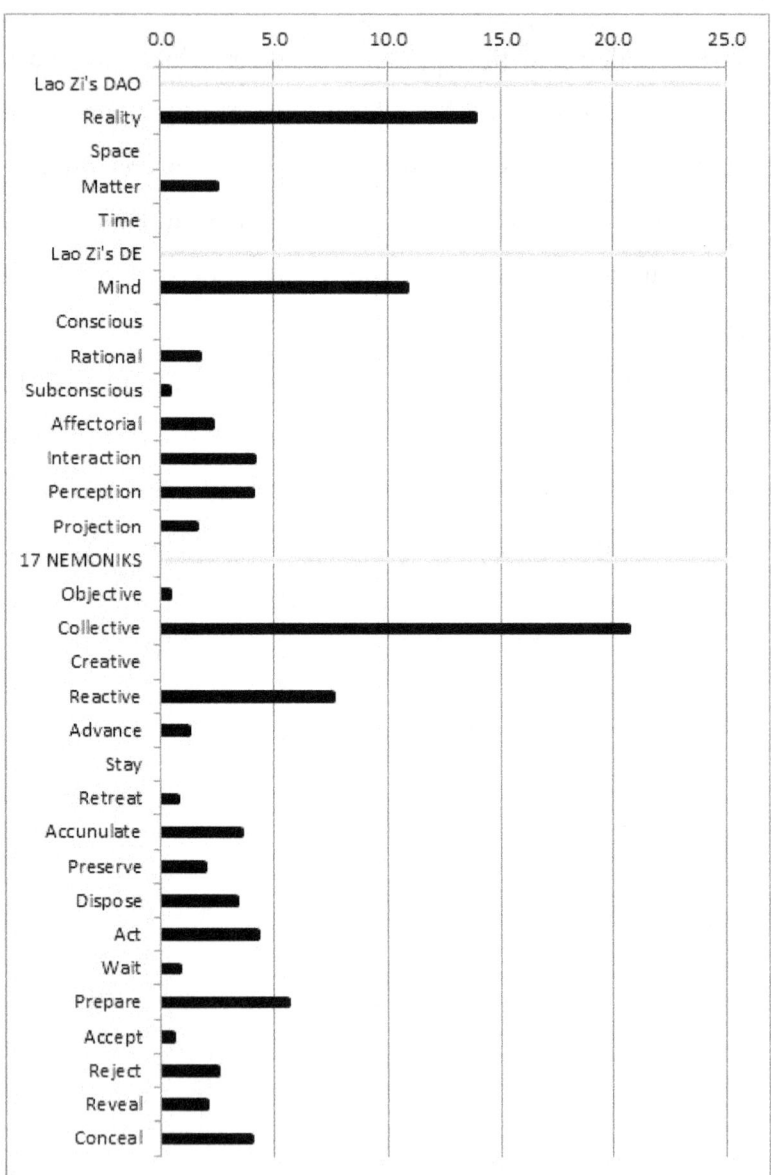

Table 5: Word-count Lao Zi's *Dao De Jing* in %.[i]

Table 5 illustrates that Lao Zi's *Dao De Jing* fits within the nemonik template. The percentage of words in Lao Zi's *Dao De Jing* associated with the nemonik template indicates the synchrony of his manuscript and nemonik thinking. In accord, the word-count for the section *Dao* or Physics is 16.3%, while for the section *De* or Psychology that count is 24.8%. Those results support the notion that in Lao Zi's philosophy, physics is the basis for psychology. Table 5 shows that Lao Zi concentrated on matter, while ignoring the concepts of space and time in his discussion of reality.

Rational thinking is associated with conscious thinking. Affectorial thinking occurs subconsciously and therefore we do not know how that way of thinking works. We only perceive the results of affectional thinking in our conscious as affecters. Hence, there is no 'knowledge' associated with affectorial thinking.

Although, Lao Zi seems to differentiate between rational thinking (1.7%) and affectorial thinking (2.2%), he did not divide explicitly the mind in a conscious and subconscious part. Furthermore, he did not mention the creative mindmode as a crucial component for success. This gap in the understanding of the mind was only filled recently by Edward de Bono's *Lateral Thinking*. Furthermore, a relatively large part of *Dao De Jing* is about the collective mindmode

(20.6%). However, that part addresses predominantly the leadership of a collective.

The results presented in Table 5 support the notion that the nemonik template provides a valid and reliable structure for cognitive psychology and nemonik thinking.

CONCLUSION

This is the last step on your 2,500 years journey back to the physics and psychology of ancient China. One has to understand nature in order to survive. Therefore, Lao Zi proposes that the *Way of Nature* or physics should be the basis for the *Way of People* or psychology. In his philosophy, the *Way of Nature* or the simply *the Way*, is the origin, force, substance, and principle of the Universe (Schade, Glossary Nemonik Thinking, 2016).

Every time the Way returns to Nothingness (14).

In its manifestation of Nothingness, the Way is the origin of the Universe. By definition, Nothingness cannot increase or decrease, because there is nothing to change it with. You cannot have more or less of Nothingness, without having something else. Nothingness cannot change. It is the immutable foundation and eternal constant of the Universe.

The One generated the Two (42).

In the beginning of the Universe, something must have been created from nothing. Otherwise, there would have been something before that creation. In that case, it has to be explained where that something came from and so on. Lao

Zi solves that fundamental riddle of the Universe. He suggests that Nothingness was divided into two equal, but opposing parts, called Existence and Non-existence). Even after the creation of Existence and Non-existence), Nothingness did not change. The Universe is part of a sum-zero creation, because the sum of the Universe remains nothing forever.[ii]

> *All-things carry Yin on their back*
> *and carry Yang in their arms.*
> *Their balance creates*
> *vital energy that restores harmony (42).*

Lao Zi explains that Yin and Yang are reflections of Non-existence) and Existence in our reality. Although *Dao De Jing* is written in a poetic style, there is nothing mystical about Lao Zi's ideas. Nowadays, we just use different labels for his concepts. For example, the fundamental balance between Yin and Yang is indicated by the mathematical equal-sign ($=$), which is fundamental to all sciences. Without accepting Lao Zi's idea of a balanced Universe, we would even have no arithmetic.[iii]

> *Do not walk through the hills*
> *in order to meet rhinoceroses and tigers (50).*

The sum of Existence and Non-existence) is Nothingness. Nothingness cannot change. Therefore, any imbalance between Existence (Yang) and Non-existence) (Yin) will evoke inevitably a correction that will restore Nothingness. The irresistible force Qi will restore the Yin-Yang balance by destroying any extremes of Yin and Yang.[2] It will level the highest mountains with the lowest valleys. Hence, all extremes are places of death. Sages will avoid such places of death. Therefore, Lao Zi derived the *Way of People* from the *Way of Nature*.

> *Obtain what you seek and*
> *escape what you suffer (62).*

The aim of Lao Zi's *Dao De Jing* is success, rather than winning. Success is to obtain what you seek and to escape what you suffer. Therefore, it is goal oriented, which fosters freedom, alignment, compassion, allies, and win-win strategies. In contrast, winning is defeating opponents in competition. Therefore, winning is conflict oriented, which fosters aggression, control, effort, force, and win-lose strategies. Winning creates counterproductive extremes.

---

[2] Qi or Chi.

Some people might win all competitions without ever being successful, because they do not focus on obtaining what they seek and escaping what they suffer. It is like climbing the mast of the sinking Titanic. They might win, but they will still drown.

> *The Way of Nature has no favourites.*
> *It is always with*
> *the competent people (79).*

Nature does not give humanity a choice. Good or evil, the balancing force of Qi turns inevitably all extremes into places of death. Therefore, sages will foster simplicity, rather than extremism. Consequently, they will nurture Lao Zi's three treasures. His compassion, frugality, and humbleness inhibit the extremes caused by strive, waste, and arrogance. Furthermore, sages curb their desires to accumulate, because extreme differences between the poor and rich will tear their collectives apart. Such a catastrophe to their support-system would threaten their chance of success.

Action and effort are also likely to create dangerous extremes, because those behaviours are like swimming upstream. Any need for action or effort indicates opposition to the unstoppable force Qi that is balancing Yin and Yang. Those opposing Qi will sooner or later run out of energy. Therefore, sages avoid great actions and efforts by aligning with the Way and using its natural forces to their advantage. They do not swim upstream, but go with the flow.

> *Those who are educated*
> *do not know (81).*

I know that this sounds strange, but I ask you to think about it. Before rejecting Lao Zi's philosophy as romantic nonsense, we should evaluate the current state of humanity. Reality shows that education infects people with the deadly cognitive CS7-virus. The resulting stereotype is a semi-rational thinker who aims to win by advancing, accumulating, acting, rejecting, and concealing.

The educated are likely to fail, because they are conditioned to win. Therefore, they are biased towards the five previously mentioned nemoniks. However, those nemoniks divide humanity, while humanity needs to be united in order to survive. As a consequence of the educational bias, humanity is facing overpopulation, dwindling resources, global pollution, climate change, and ongoing warfare. Each of those problems is manmade and could easily destroy humanity (Schade, Education Kills Humanity, 2016).

Lao Zi's brilliant *Dao De Jing* is more relevant than ever. His ideas create a unifying force that reaches peacefully across the boundaries of gender, race, religion, spiritualism, ideology, and science. Reality shows that a chronic misunderstanding of Lao Zi's *Dao De Jing* has done considerable damage to humanity and our environment. We are running out of time, because Qi is already restoring the Yin-Yang balance. We have to decide whether that new balance will be with or without us. Remember, in order to achieve success, Lao Zi's *Way of Nature* is our *Way for the Future*.

APPENDICES

INDEX

abandon..61, 62, 77
ability... 23
abnormal.. 58, 63
above..43, 51, 81
accept..43, 51, 55, 58, 78, 80
accountant... 33
accumulate.............................25, 55, 61, 67, 74, 90, 91
achieve...................... 35, 40, 44, 45, 47, 57, 59, 73, 76
action...21, 23, 27, 31, 35, 37, 40, 42, 43, 44, 46, 50, 51, 54, 58, 59, 62, 65, 67, 71, 72, 73, 74, 75, 76, 77, 81, 90, 91
admire...22, 54, 58, 67, 76, 77, 82
adoration..37, 54, 79, 82
advance...25, 43, 65, 91
affair....................23, 33, 34, 51, 62, 72, 75, 77, 79, 82, 83
affecters..39, 59, 60, 85
agreement... 50, 71
All-things... 19, 21, 22, 23, 26, 27, 32, 50, 62, 64, 71, 72, 77, 88
ambition.. 34
analysing.. 74
Ancients......................31, 42, 52, 53, 63, 65, 71, 75, 80, 82
angry... 65, 71
apply.. 34, 83
arithmetic.. 88
arms are bared... 50
army................................. 31, 50, 52, 53, 57, 58, 65, 66, 69
arrogant............ 40, 46, 58, 62, 63, 64, 67, 76, 80, 81, 82, 90
artificial... 49
associate... 55
attachment.. 76, 77
attack...23, 57, 58, 63, 65
authority... 58
awareness..36, 38, 39
baby... 34
backwards..24, 35, 44
bad... 42

bamboo counting sticks...34
basket of dirt..77
beauty.. 45, 56
begin..24, 32, 50, 77
behind...43, 51, 81
beliefs.. 39, 60
below..43, 51, 81
bend.. 36, 45, 46, 63, 80
beneficial............... 20, 26, 31, 37, 53, 54, 71, 73, 74, 76, 79, 82
benevolence.................................... 21, 50, 54, 61, 70, 75, 79
betray...37, 53, 82
big... 50, 57
birds of prey..34
black..41
bland... 20, 33
boast...43, 46, 52, 58, 62, 63, 80, 81, 82
body... 56, 57
bow..22
brainstorming..59
break...22, 26, 50, 77
bright... 24, 35, 42, 44, 63
brilliant................. 40, 46, 62, 63, 64, 69, 76, 77, 78, 80, 81, 82
bureaucracy.. 50, 79
burglar... 54, 79
business people...56
calm...33
careful... 42, 77
carriage.. 20, 26, 56
certain..57
chariot...73
cheap cloth... 35, 83
Chi..89, 90, 92
chicken..56
chief...41, 65, 71, 78
chiefs of fools.. 41, 78
children... 32, 42
China..87

nemonik-thinking.org

claim...	57, 72
clear...	19, 21, 57, 74
cleverness...	50, 54, 79
climate change...	91
clumsy...	36, 45
cognitive dissonance...	38, 157
cold...	54, 79
collective...	37, 48, 49, 85, 86, 90
companions of death...	22, 26, 50
companions of life...	22, 26, 50
compassion...	54, 61, 79, 80, 89, 90
competence...	22, 31, 32, 33, 34, 35, 42, 49, 51, 52, 58, 62, 63, 65, 67, 68, 69, 70, 71, 74, 75, 78, 82, 90
complete...	18
conceal...	35, 46, 81, 83, 91
concentration...	30, 36, 48
Confucius...	49, 149, 150
confused...	46, 50, 53, 57, 64, 67, 70, 79, 80
conqueror...	65, 71
conscious...	30, 36, 38, 39, 48, 85
conserving...	31, 69
constant...	40, 64, 76
contempt...	76
continuous...	20
contraction...	37, 72
control...	77
corps de esprit...	52
country...	33, 37, 51, 52, 53, 54, 55, 56, 61, 78, 80, 82
courage...	31, 61, 69, 74
creation...	87, 88
creative...	39, 48, 59, 60, 85
criminal...	53, 58
crowned...	32
CS7-virus...	91
cultivate...	33
cup...	20, 26
custom...	56

cut	42, 63, 77
danger	32, 40, 53, 64, 68, 74
Dao De Jing	11, 13, 14, 84, 85, 88, 89, 91, 92
Dao	13, 85
dare	22, 27, 31, 37, 43, 54, 58, 59, 62, 63, 65, 68, 69, 74, 77
dazzle	42, 63
de Bono, Edward	59, 60, 85
De	13, 85
death	31, 32, 47, 51, 56, 58, 59, 69
decay	79
decision-making	74
delicacies	54
depleted	24, 33, 70
desire	23, 37, 39, 42, 43, 46, 51, 53, 54, 56, 57, 60, 62, 67, 68, 72, 77, 81, 82, 83, 90
desolate	18
detachment	76
development	37, 46, 47, 53, 62, 63, 80, 81, 82
die	22, 26, 34, 50, 56, 61, 62
different	34, 41, 56, 57, 70
difficult	37, 42, 45, 53, 54, 55, 67, 76, 77, 82
dim	24, 44
disaster	64
disgrace	35, 41, 56, 62, 63, 68
disgusting	46, 57, 62, 81
disorder	22, 27, 50, 76, 79
display	42, 46, 54, 58, 62, 63, 80, 81, 82
dispose	25, 70
dissatisfaction	56
dissipating	42
distress	56
distrust	52
divide	53
dog	56
doors	20, 26, 41, 79
drift along	35
dry	20, 22, 26, 50

dust..22, 27, 76
dwelling..56, 58
dyslexia... 40
Earth..18, 19, 20, 21, 26
easy...20, 34, 45, 76, 77, 83
educated.. 37, 42, 79, 91
effective.. 19
effort.. 38, 52, 53, 54, 72, 73, 76, 89, 90
Einstein, Albert...25, 48
elect..43, 51
elusive...24, 44
embroidered coloured silk..................................... 43, 52, 62, 81
emotions... 39, 60
Emperor..18, 32, 44
employing people..52, 65, 71
empty................18, 21, 22, 24, 33, 35, 42, 45, 46, 51, 62, 70, 80
end...24, 77, 79
endure...21, 55, 61, 68, 74
energy.. 24, 34, 68, 72
engage... 65, 71
enjoy.. 56
enlighten..53, 82
enough.................... 22, 24, 33, 34, 44, 52, 54, 64, 67, 68, 70, 72
environment... 21
equal-sign.. 88
escape...31, 75, 89
eternal constant... 87
evil... 64
example.. 41
excess..58, 63
exchange.. 79
execution..58, 59, 73
exhausted...21, 35, 45, 46, 68, 70, 80
exhaustive... 13, 14, 25, 27, 41, 43, 46
Existence..19, 20, 26, 32, 45, 49, 88, 89
expand...37, 72
exploit..32, 68, 73

nemonik-thinking.org

extravangance..68, 76, 79
extreme........................31, 38, 63, 64, 66, 67, 69, 70, 76, 79, 90
fail..68, 71, 72, 73, 77, 79
fame..23, 68, 75
family...50, 79
Father of the Multitude...32
favour...31, 56, 71, 90
fear...19, 20, 21, 52, 57, 58, 59, 72
feet...77
female..34, 40, 55, 63
few...35, 56, 59, 73, 74, 76, 82, 83
field...50, 62
filial piety...54, 61, 79
filling..19, 54, 67, 74
firm..34, 46, 61, 62, 81
first of the world..62
fish..58, 82
five colours..45, 54
five flavours...45, 55
five tones..45, 54
flattery..41, 56
flaw..33, 49
fold..77
food................................20, 33, 43, 51, 52, 56, 57, 63, 81
force...58, 63, 87, 89, 90, 91
forever.......................18, 19, 20, 21, 33, 40, 44, 45, 62, 64
forget...34
fortune..31, 58, 63, 75
foundation..52, 55, 61, 73
fragile..22, 26, 50, 77
front..43, 51, 81
frugal...55, 61, 69, 80, 90
fruit...41, 78
fruitless flowers..41, 78
fullness..35, 45, 68
future..41, 78
gain...68, 75

nemonik-thinking.org

generate... 32, 68, 73
generous... 61
genius... 38, 154, 155, 156
give... 22, 67, 70
glare... 22, 27, 76
goal... 49, 57, 65, 66, 89, 157
goals... 30, 75
good... 24, 31, 32, 40, 42, 45, 63, 67, 74
goodness... 22, 31, 42, 45, 70, 71, 74, 75, 80
govern... 51
grandeur... 68, 76, 79
grass... 22, 26, 50
Great Road... 50, 72
great...20, 24, 32, 34, 35, 41, 50, 52, 53, 56, 68, 71, 72, 73, 76, 78, 79, 83
greatest form... 35, 45
greatest sound... 35, 45
greatest square... 35, 45
greatest talent... 35, 45
greatness... 73, 76
Greatness... 20, 26
groupthink... 38, 157
grow... 21, 22, 26, 58, 73, 77, 79
guest... 42, 43, 73
Guilford, Joy Paul... 59
happy... 43, 51, 57
hard... 21, 22, 23, 26, 44, 50, 64, 73, 79
harmful... 31, 32, 38, 43, 45, 51, 55, 69, 71, 76, 81
harmony... 22, 26, 34, 40, 88
hate... 71, 76
hear... 24, 33, 35, 44, 56, 70
heaviness... 73
height... 77
hesitant... 42
hiding... 31, 69
high... 20, 22, 45, 50, 51, 52
hoard... 67, 68

hold... 46, 59, 68, 72, 73, 77, 80
holistic..11
home...21, 35, 40, 44
honour............................... 41, 46, 52, 62, 63, 80, 81, 82
horse...32
host... 43, 65
hot...79
household...33, 50, 53, 79
humble...61, 62, 80, 90
hundred valleys..51
hunger...51
hypocrisy.. 50, 79
I...18, 20, 23, 27, 33, 35, 43, 44, 47, 53, 56, 57, 59, 61, 62, 64, 65, 68, 72, 73, 80, 83
ideas... 39, 48, 59, 88, 91, 154, 156
ignoble...52
inaudible... 19, 24, 44
incompetence.. 31, 32, 35, 69, 70
independent..18
infancy... 52, 64
inferior... 32, 56
infinite... 19, 44
information..25
information overload...38
information..24
insects...34
institution... 34, 54, 56
insubstantial.. 19, 24, 44
insufficient... 35, 36, 45
interaction..13, 14, 30, 41, 43, 46
interfere..42, 63, 68, 72
intersection..55
intuitions.. 39, 60
invisible.. 19, 24, 44
irrational..39
jade..31, 67, 68, 83
justice...50, 52, 53, 79

karma ... 41
kill ... 31, 57, 69, 74
kindness ... 76
King ... 19, 20, 26, 51, 52, 62, 78, 80
knotted cords ... 56
know ... 18, 22, 32, 33, 34, 35, 37, 40, 41, 42, 44, 50, 52, 53, 54, 58, 63, 64, 67, 68, 70, 72, 73, 74, 76, 78, 79, 82, 91
koans ... 40
Lao Zi ... 11, 13, 60, 84, 85, 87, 88, 89, 90, 91, 92, 153
large ... 56, 68, 76
laugh ... 35
law ... 53, 58
lax ... 58
leading ... 43, 51, 52, 62, 65, 71, 75, 81, 83, 86
learn ... 35, 40, 44, 77
learning ... 36, 74
leftover food ... 46, 62, 81
life ... 31, 32, 40, 51, 55, 61, 64, 68, 69, 71, 73, 75, 79
lightness ... 73
listening ... 19, 24, 31, 33, 44, 69, 70
live on ... 21, 31, 34, 51, 58, 69, 74, 79
look ... 19, 24, 33, 44, 70
loss ... 33, 34, 35, 62, 67, 68, 72, 73, 75, 77
love ... 57, 58, 68, 70, 82
low ... 20, 22, 45, 50, 51, 52, 55, 56, 65, 71, 83
loyalty ... 50
male ... 34, 40, 55, 63
manifest ... 77
Marquis ... 19, 52, 62
master carpenter ... 59, 73
master ... 23, 24
matching with nature ... 52, 65, 71
matter ... 25, 27, 67, 69, 70, 72, 85
meddle ... 79
mediocre ... 35
meditation ... 39
merge ... 19, 20, 24, 26, 33, 42, 44, 56

merit.. 46, 62, 63, 66, 80, 81, 82
mill-stone of jade...32
mind...13, 14, 18, 19, 20, 30, 31, 36, 38, 39, 41, 43, 45, 46, 54, 55, 57, 59, 65, 66, 67, 69, 70, 72, 74, 78, 80, 81, 85
mindmode
   ---collective...37, 48, 49, 85
   ---creative..39, 48, 59, 85
   ---objective... .... 36, 48
   ---reactive... 40, 60
mindsets... 38, 60
ministers...32
misfortune...40, 51, 57, 58, 62, 63, 64, 65, 66, 67, 75, 76, 78, 80
mistake..77
modesty... 43, 54, 56, 62, 82
Mother... 21, 32, 55, 57, 61
moving without moving... 65
much...41, 56, 67, 70
mud.. 42, 74
music... 20, 33
Mysterious Female..21
name... .... 18, 19, 21, 24, 32, 35, 40, 44, 52, 68
named...18, 19, 21, 23, 24, 44
nameless..18, 21, 24, 62
nature...20, 22, 26, 27, 32, 35, 40, 44, 51, 55, 61, 64, 66, 68, 69, 71, 75, 77, 82, 83
neighbour..42
nemonik template....................................11, 12, 14, 15, 85, 86
nemoniks....13, 43, 59, 65, 66, 67, 69, 70, 72, 74, 78, 80, 81, 91
net of nature... ....22, 75
Newton, Sir Isaac...48
noble..32, 52
Non-action....................................37, 53, 54, 72, 73, 74, 76, 77, 82
Non-existence... ....20, 26, 45, 88, 89
normal...63
nothing..22, 23, 47, 55, 59, 61, 69, 75
Nothingness... 19, 23, 24, 44, 87, 88, 89

nemonik-thinking.org

objective	48
obligate	71
obscure	24, 35, 44
obtain	31, 32, 45, 54, 55, 56, 67, 75, 77, 89
One	19, 21, 24, 26, 44, 46, 52, 80, 87
opinion	42
organisation	53, 64, 74
organizing	74
origin	18, 19, 20, 21, 26, 49, 87
orphans and widowers	52
orthodox	23, 71
overcome	22, 23, 34, 55, 58, 63, 64, 71, 73
overpopulation	91
overthrown	52
palace	50, 62
paradox	42, 45, 51, 78, 80
perception	41, 43
perfect	24, 34, 53
perish	23, 58
physics	13, 85, 87
plan	22, 51, 75, 77, 83
Planck, Max	48
planning	74
pleasing	41, 42, 45, 79
plenty	22, 33, 70
pollution	91
position	32, 50, 51, 52, 55, 65, 71
positioning	74, 149, 150, 152, 159
possess	32, 50, 55, 57, 61, 68, 70, 73
power	31, 34, 38, 54, 58, 63, 68
precedence	34, 83
prepare	27, 55, 61, 74
preserve	25, 46, 63, 69, 80
principle	19, 49, 52, 53, 65, 71, 87
prioritizing	74
proactivity	75
procrastination	75

profit.. 54, 79
profound virtue... 32, 53, 68, 73
prohibition... 53, 58
projection... 41, 46
promises.. 76
propriety... 50
protection... 32
psychology.. 13, 85, 86, 87
pure.. 19, 21, 35, 41, 54, 63, 72
purpose............... 21, 23, 26, 43, 50, 51, 57, 71, 73, 76
quiet.. 19, 21
race horses.. 49
raise.. 22, 56
rash.. 63, 73, 76
reality
---............13, 14, 18, 25, 27, 36, 39, 41, 48, 59, 60, 85, 88, 91
---constructed.. 18
---external... 18, 30
---extrasensory... 18, 30, 48
---internal.. 18, 38
---scientific... 18
---sensory..................... 18, 25, 36, 43, 46, 48, 49, 78, 80, 81
---simulated... 18
---supernatural... 18
reason..................................... 22, 31, 32, 36, 39, 48, 49, 69
rebound.. 58
rebuke.. 41, 56
receive.. 46, 67, 70, 73, 80
regard......................... 46, 55, 61, 62, 63, 77, 80, 81, 82
reject...37, 43, 50, 54, 55, 58, 61, 62, 67, 68, 69, 76, 78, 79, 82, 91
relaxation... 38, 39
rely.. 42, 72, 73
reorganized... 11, 14
repair.. 77
resistance... 65, 66
resource.................... 43, 52, 62, 63, 69, 70, 78, 81, 91

respect..21, 37, 41
rest..57, 77
retreat...25, 43, 65, 66
return...19, 20, 23, 24, 27, 32, 34, 38, 40, 44, 53, 54, 56, 57, 61, 63, 64, 76, 79, 81, 87
reveal..46, 80
rhinoceros...31, 32, 69, 89
rich..34, 67
righteousness...54, 61, 79
rigid...42, 63
risk-management...74
river...23, 42, 51
rock...68
rolling up the sleeves...65
room...20, 26, 67
root..23, 27, 55, 61, 64, 76
rough..24, 35, 44
rule...37, 52, 53, 54, 55, 58, 61, 69, 75, 82
safety..79
sage...27, 32, 35, 37, 38, 40, 41, 42, 43, 44, 46, 51, 53, 54, 55, 58, 61, 63, 66, 67, 69, 71, 72, 73, 76, 77, 78, 79, 80, 81, 82, 83, 89, 90
sanctuary..32
satisfaction..56, 57
saying...35, 51, 53, 56, 63, 65, 78, 80
scare..58
scatter..77
science..48, 88, 91
scorpion..34
sea...23, 51, 57
see...24, 33, 35, 40, 44, 56, 68, 70
seek..31, 51, 75, 89
seize...34, 59, 77
self-interest...66
selfishness..43, 54, 56, 62, 83
semiconscious...30
senses...43

Term	Pages
shame	51, 78, 80
shapeless	19, 23, 24, 44
sharp weapon	57
sharp	42, 43, 52, 53, 57, 58, 62, 63, 67, 76, 81, 82
shortage	58
simple	22, 42, 43, 53, 54, 56, 62, 64, 75, 77, 82, 83, 90
sincerity	50
skill	36, 45, 75
Sky	18, 19, 20, 21, 26
sleep	38
small	23, 31, 42, 54, 55, 56, 64, 76, 77
soft	22, 23, 26, 34, 50, 52, 58, 64, 73
soldier	32, 58, 69
solemn	42
sovereign	34, 63, 73, 83
space	25, 27, 72, 85
speak	22, 33, 37, 41, 45, 51, 72, 74, 75, 79, 80, 82, 83
Spencer, Herbert	39
spirit	38, 54
stab	42, 63
state	50, 52, 53, 57, 58, 73, 79, 82
stay	25, 66
stop	20, 33, 37, 53, 54, 57, 58, 63, 68, 74
storehouse	50, 62
straight	35, 42, 45, 63
straw dogs	21
strength	64, 77
stress	156
strict	58
strive	22, 23, 31, 37, 43, 47, 51, 52, 54, 65, 71, 76, 80, 82, 89, 90, 149, 150, 152, 155
strong	22, 23, 26, 34, 50, 55, 58, 61, 64, 79
stubborn	57
stupid	57
subconscious	18, 30, 38, 39, 85
substance	19, 23, 25, 44, 73, 87

success...13, 23, 30, 43, 46, 51, 58, 62, 63, 65, 67, 68, 72, 74, 75, 77, 79, 83, 85, 89, 90, 92
suffering..31, 56, 57, 67, 75, 89
superior..22, 32, 35, 50, 71
surplus................................ 43, 46, 52, 57, 58, 63, 67, 80, 81
surprise... 52, 53
sweet dew.. 21
sweeten... 56
sword...32, 43, 52, 63, 69, 81
taste.. 20, 33, 73, 76
tax.. 51
teach...47, 59, 70, 72, 74, 82
thick... 41, 78
thief..43, 52, 54, 63, 79, 81
thin..41, 50, 78
thinking
   ---affectorial.................................. 13, 38, 39, 40, 59, 60, 85
   ---critical.. 36
   ---divergent... 60
   ---lateral... 60, 85
   ---nemonik...................................13, 36, 39, 75, 85, 86
   ---rational.. 11, 13, 36, 39, 48, 49, 85
thirty spokes.. 20, 26
thorn.. 58
thoroughness.. 71
three in ten... 31, 69
three treasures..61, 80, 90
Three... 19, 26
tiger... 31, 32, 69, 89
time management.. 75
time...25, 27, 72, 74, 85, 87, 92
tiptoe..46, 62, 81
titles.. 53, 74
tool... 56, 57
tower.. 77
trail... 33
training... 75

Term	Pages
tranquil	24, 53, 55, 62, 63
tranquillity	23, 54, 55, 63, 64, 66, 70, 73, 76
travel	20, 33, 35, 40, 44, 73
treasure	65, 66
tree	22, 26, 50, 77
triumph	36, 45, 61
true	35, 42, 45, 63, 75, 79, 80, 81
trust	42, 52, 76
twist	46, 80
Two	19, 26, 87
ugly	45
unchanging	18
understand	19, 34, 35, 49, 83
undivided	18
unfolded	77
Universe	20, 26, 87, 88
unorthodox	23
use	20, 22, 24, 26, 31, 33, 37, 42, 47, 50, 51, 52, 53, 54, 55, 56, 57, 58, 59, 61, 70, 72, 75, 77, 82
vague	42
Valley Spirit	21
valley	19, 20, 23, 35, 41, 42, 64
victory	57
village	33, 57
violent	47, 59
viper	34
virtue	21, 22, 32, 33, 34, 35, 38, 50, 52, 53, 55, 61, 64, 65, 71
vital energy	22, 26, 31, 52, 64, 88
void	19, 44
wait	27, 74
war horses	50
war	50, 65, 71, 91
warden	34
warrior	65, 71
waste	90
water	22, 23, 58, 71, 82
Way for the Future	92

Way of Nature... 13, 22, 31, 70, 71, 87, 89, 90, 92
Way of People... 13, 31, 70, 71, 87, 89
Way...18, 19, 20, 21, 22, 23, 24, 26, 31, 32, 33, 35, 37, 40, 41, 42, 43, 44, 46, 49, 50, 51, 52, 53, 54, 55, 57, 61, 62, 63, 64, 66, 68, 70, 71, 72, 75, 78, 79, 81, 82
weak... 22, 23, 26, 34, 37, 41, 50, 58, 64, 77, 79
wealth... 53, 62, 67, 68, 75
weapon... 32, 53, 56, 58, 65, 66, 69, 82
weaver... 34
white... 41
window... 35, 40, 44
win-lose strategies... 89
winning... 43, 50, 65, 66, 89, 90, 91
win-win strategies... 89
wise... 40
withdrawing... 66
word... 20, 33, 34, 41, 45, 51, 78, 80, 83
word-count... 84, 85
work... 73, 76
world...18, 19, 20, 22, 23, 26, 31, 32, 33, 34, 35, 40, 41, 42, 43, 44, 45, 46, 49, 51, 52, 53, 54, 55, 57, 58, 62, 63, 64, 68, 70, 71, 72, 73, 74, 75, 76, 78, 80, 82
Yang... 22, 26, 88, 89, 90
Yin... 22, 26, 88, 89, 90
Yin-Yang balance... 89, 92
yourself... 33, 66

BIBLIOGRAPHY

Schade, A. (2016). *Dictionary Nemonik Thinking.* nemonik-thinking.org.

Schade, A. (2016). *Education Kills Humanity.* nemonik-thinking.org.

Schade, A. (2016). *Global Warming is the Solution.* nemonik-thinking.org.

Schade, A. (2016). *Glossary Nemonik Thinking.* nemonik-thinking.org.

Schade, A. (2016). *Lao Tzu's Tao Te Ching.* nemonik-thinking.org.

Schade, A. (2016). *Lao Zi's Dao De Jing.* nemonik-thinking.org.

Schade, A. (2016). *Lao Zi's Dao De Jing Explained.* nemonik-thinking.org.

Schade, A. (2016). *Lao Zi's Dao De Jing for Nemonik Thinkers.*

Schade, A. (2016). *Lao Zi's Dao De Jing: Meta-translation.* nemonik-thinking.org.

Schade, A. (2016). *Think Smarter with Nemonik Thinking.* nemonik-thinking.org.

Schade, A. (2016). *Think Smarter with Nemonik Thinking.* nemonik-thinking.org.

Schade, A. (planned 2017). *Lao Zi's Dao De Jing: Chinese-English Dictionary.* nemonik-thinking.org.

Schade, A. (planned 2017). *Lao Zi's True Dao De Jing*. nemonik-thinking.org.

Schade, A. (planned 2017). *Sun Zi's The Art of War*. nemonik-thinking.org.

Schade, A. (planned 2017). *The Unreal Reality*. nemonik-thinking.org.

Schade, A. (planned 2017). *The Unreal Reality* (1 ed.). nemonik-thinking.org.

LIST OF TABLES

Table 1: Nemonik Template. 12
Table 2: Nemonik Template for *Dao De Jing*. 15
Table 3: Diagram of Reality. 18
Table 4: Diagram of the Mind. 30
Table 5: Word-count Lao Zi's *Dao De Jing* in %. 84

GLOSSARY

Accept—perceptual nemonik that prompts the mind to accept the incoming information as a true description of the sensory reality. One can adopt a strict or lax decision criterion. See Perception.

Accumulate—material nemonik that prompts the mind to increase the amount of matter that is under control. See Matter.

Act—temporal nemonik that prompts the mind to change or move matter in space and time. See Time.

Advance—spatial nemonik that prompts the mind to decrease the distance to the goal. See Space.

Affecters—mental signals that are generated by subconscious affectorial thinking, which influence the conscious without explaining the underlying subconscious processes. Affecters do not rely on conscious reasoning or facts, and therefore, they are by definition non-rational and illogical. However, affecters are sometimes rationalised. Affecters can be divided into creative affecters and reactive affecters. Affecters include beliefs, desires, discoveries, emotions, fantasies, habits, heuristics, ideas, impulses, innovations, insights, inspirations, intuitions, inventions, novelties, reactions, reflexes, routines, skills, etc. See Affectorial thinking.

Affectorial thinking—subconscious part of nemonik thinking that deals with the unpredictable chaos of reality by generating affecters that influence the conscious. Affecters are mental signals that are generated by subconscious affectorial thinking, which influence the conscious without explaining the underlying subconscious processes. The mental processes underlying affectorial thinking are outside the conscious awareness. Hence, they cannot be observed directly and, therefore, affectorial thinking appears non-rational and irrational to the rational conscious. This is not to say that affectorial thinking is without reason. We just do not know the underlying processes, because they are hidden in the subconscious. The word 'irrational' has often been used as a negative label to discredit affectorial thinking. Furthermore, meditation, relaxation, and a silent mind foster subconscious dominance and affectorial thinking. The opposite of affectorial thinking is rational thinking. Herbert Spencer introduced the unknown and known. These, concepts underlie the division of affectorial thinking into respectively the creative (unknown) and reactive mindmodes (known). Dyslexia and koans might foster affectorial thinking. However, more research is required. In the context of Lao Zi's philosophy, affectorial thinking could be called *Yin* thinking. See Subconscious.

Aligning with harmonisations—moving in the same direction as *Qi* when this inexhaustible force is harmonising the *Yin-Yang* balance. Aligning is the second of the three fundamental alignments with the Way (*Dao*). During the harmonisation of the *Yin-Yang* balance, the unlimited force of the Way provides free energy that we can use to our advantage. Instead of rowing upstream, sages drift with the flow of the water to their destination. The natural virtue of humility is one of Lao Zi's three treasures and part of aligning with harmonisation.

Aligning with *Qi*—See Aligning with harmonisations.

Aligning with the Way—aiming for the right goals, while being in the right place, at the right time, with the right resources and in the right state of mind. This requires Non-action; Affectorial thinking; Maintaining the *Yin-Yang* balance; Aligning with Harmonisations; and Restoring the *Yin-Yang* balance.

Alignment—positioning in order to take optimal advantage of the Way (*Dao*). Alignment is the constant of the sages. See Aligning with the Way and Three fundamental alignments.

All-things(万物)—literally ten thousand things or just a great number of things. All-things refer to the myriad of organic and inorganic things that exist in the sensory reality.

Ancients(古)—sages of antiquity that Lao Zi refers to in *Dao De Jing*.

Balance—See Harmony.

Benevolence (仁)—Confucian artificial virtue that maintains imbalances in collective. In terms of Confucian philosophy, benevolence is the love for one's fellow men. To be benevolent, it is essential that we do not impose on others what we do not desire for ourselves. Benevolence is associated with a social class called *'gentleman'*. This fosters division by creating a 'them and us' mentality. See Confucius.

Bono de—See de Bono.

Chi—See Qi.

Collective mindmode—way of rational thinking that generates artificial rules, which determine the rights and obligations of individuals within a collective and makes their behaviours predictable. Collective refers to an organized group of people with a common goal such as a family, business, tribe, nation, or the entire human race.

Artificial refers to that part of the sensory reality that is manmade. The collective mindmode uses the mental order of reason to deal with the artificial order of the sensory reality. The Chinese philosopher Confucius was an important advocate of collective thinking. Collective specialists are found where proficiency in artificial rules is crucial such as in accountancy, bureaucracy, court, and government. See Rational thinking.

Compassion (慈)—affectorial sympathy for other people that inhibits competitive behaviour in order to maximize the probability of success. Compassion is one of Lao Zi's three treasures. Compassion provides courage and strength. Compassion for other people prevents counterproductive harmonisations. See Three treasures.

Competence—See *De*.

Conceal—projectional nemonik that prompts the mind to project false information to the sensory reality. See Projection.

Confucius, Kung Ciu, or Kung Chung-ni (551-479 BC)—Chinese philosopher who was one of the first to address the problems concerning the artificial rules of the collectives. He was a contemporary of Lao Zi. However, Lao Zi's philosophy diametrically opposes the ideas of Confucius. Confucius elaborated on what Lao Zi calls The Way of People (*De*). Lao Zi pointed out that The Way of Nature (*Dao*) is always superior to The Way of the People. After Confucius' death, his students compiled his ideas in a manuscript called: *The Analects*. See Collective mindmode.

Conscious—small part of the mind that is only active when that person is fully awake. The conscious is associated with awareness, concentration, learning, sensory reality, and rational thinking. See Mind.

Constant of the Sages—Alignment with the Way (*Dao*). See *Dao De Jing*.

Constant of the Universe—See Harmonisation.

Control—maintaining an imbalance between *Yin* and *Yang* that the Way (*Dao*) continuously seeks to harmonise.

Cosmos—sum of Existence and Non-existence, matter and antimatter, or our Universe and any parallel or anti-Universe.

Creative affecters—include discoveries, fantasies, ideas, innovations, insights, inspirations, inventions, novelties, etc.

Creative mindmode—way of affectorial thinking that deals with the unknown or inexperienced aspects of reality by generating creative affecters. The seventeen nemoniks are memory prompts and markers for mind mapping that foster the associative processes of the creative mindmode. The creative mindmode uses mental disorganisation or chaos to deal with the chaos of reality. For example, brainstorming is a random process that fosters creativity. The creative mindmode provides new experiences and, therefore, it moves people outside their comfort zone. Joy Paul Guilford and Edward de Bono extended our knowledge about creative thinking. Guilford introduced *'divergent thinking'* and de Bono *'lateral thinking'*. Creative specialists are found where originality is crucial such as in art, design, invention, research, etc. See Affectorial thinking.

Dao (道)—means literally 'road, path, way, or pathway'. However, in the context of Lao Zi's philosophy, *Dao* means *The Way of Nature* or simply *The Way*. The Way is the core of Lau Tzu's philosophy and is the origin, principle, substance, and force of the Universe. Nowadays, we would call the study of the Way *Physics*. The Way explains the Universe, the meaning of life and our place in nature. The Way is the highest of Lao Zi's Four Greatnesses that constitute the Universe. The Way is constant, elusive, eternal, infinite, unstoppable, and neutral. It has so many manifestations that it cannot be given a single name. Although water can manifest itself as ice or steam, its true essence remains water. Similarly, the Way has different manifestations, but its true essence remains the Way. It may manifest itself as a soft rain on a summer afternoon, a spinning electron, lightening, a tornado, an earthquake, a waterfall, a supernova, a black hole and so on. Hence, Lao Zi uses many synonyms and metaphors to describe those manifestations of the Way. The Way of Lao Zi is based on the unchangeable rules of the Universe and is natural, eternal, unchangeable, and objective. In contrast, the way of Confucius is based on manmade rules and is artificial, temporary, changeable, and subjective. Therefore, Lao Zi's Way of Nature is of a higher order than the Confucian Way of People. The Way is bound to maintain the cosmological constancy of Nothingness and, therefore, will always harmonise the *Yin-Yang* balance. The Way becomes clearly detectable as the harmonising force *Qi* during the harmonisation of the *Yin-Yang* balance. After each harmonisation, the Way will be undetectable again and return to nothingness. *Dao* is a phonetic notation of a Chinese pictograph and, therefore, it is alternatively spelled as *Tao*. See *Dao De Jing*.

Dao De Jing (道德經)—book written by Lao Zi about two-and-half thousand years ago. *Dao De Jing* means a classic (*Jing*) about the Way of Nature (*Dao*) and the Way of

People (*De*). Nowadays, we call the Way of the Nature *Physics*, while the Way of the people has become *Psychology*. Thus, the modern meaning of *Dao De Jing* is: *A Classic about Physics and Psychology*. Lao Zi summarises succinctly the purpose of *Dao De Jing* with a quotation of the ancient sages: *"Use it to obtain what you seek and to escape what you suffer."* The title *Dao De Jing* is a phonetic notation of Chinese pictographs and, therefore, it is alternatively spelled as *DaoDeJing, Daodejing, Dao De Jing, TaoTeChing, Taoteching,* etc.

Daoism—philosophical and religious system with millions of followers that maintains that one should follow the rules of nature, rather than the rules of the collective. For that reason, one should empty the mind of all doctrines and knowledge. In that way, one will return to the Oneness of *Dao* and exceed all distinctions, even the one between life and death. Some *Dao*ists consider Lao Zi to be a divine person. However, Lao Zi's Four Greatnesses do not include the *Divine* and there is no indication in *Dao De Jing* that Lao Zi saw himself as a divine being.

De (德)—means literally *virtue*. In the context of Lao Zi's *Dao De Jing*, it means the Way of the People. Nowadays, we call studying the way of the people *Psychology*. Furthermore, Lao Zi's concept of virtue diametrically opposes that of his contemporary Confucius. Whereas Lao Zi's virtue is based on natural laws (objective mindmode), Confucius' virtue is based on artificial rules (collective mindmode). Hence, Laozian sages align with the Way of Nature and foster natural virtue. Confucian sages align with the Way of People and foster artificial virtue. *De* is a phonetic notation of a Chinese pictograph and, therefore, it is alternatively spelled as *Te*. See *Dao De Jing*.

de Bono, Edward (1933--)—Maltese consultant, inventor, and physician who introduced lateral thinking in 1970. Lateral thinking is a way of creative thinking that reformulates problems and looks at them from different perspectives in order to find solutions. Furthermore, Edward de Bono advocates the inclusion of thinking in the school curriculum. Nemonik thinking providers the tools for lateral thinking. See Creative mindmode.

Desolate (萧)—state of the Way (*Dao*) prior to the formation of the Universe.

Dispose—material nemonik that prompts the mind to decrease the amount matter that is under control. See Matter.

Earth (地)—third of the four Greatnesses that constitute the Universe. "The Way is Great; the Sky is Great; the Earth is Great; and the King is also Great" (Lao Zi).

Effort (事)—strenuous and vigorous exertion to achieve success. In Lao Zi's philosophy, effort is a compass that shows you how to negotiate life's dangerous rapids. When you have to use effort to achieve success, you know that you are opposing the Way (*Dao*).

Einstein, Albert (1879-1955)—Swiss scientist who published in 1905 three papers that revolutionized Newtonian physics. The papers addressed the electromagnetic radiation of light, special theory of relativity, and the idea that mass and energy are equivalent. Einstein formulated the theory of relativity, which holds that it is impossible to determine absolute motion. This theory did lead to the notion of a four-dimensional space-time continuum. At Princeton, Einstein attempted to unify the laws of physics. His well-known formula $E = mc^2$ shows the relationship between energy (E), mass (m) and the constant speed of light (c). Given that the speed of light is 300,000 kilometres a second, c-squared is a very large number. Einstein's formula shows that infinitesimal amounts of matter contain immense amounts of energy. His formula shows also that energy is equivalent to matter and vice versa. This equivalence is in accord with Lao Zi's idea of Oneness. Furthermore, Einstein synthesized Newton's thesis that light comprised small particles with Young's antithesis that light was a wave.

Emptiness (冲)—manifestation of the Way (*Dao*) prior to the formation of the Universe.

Energy of the Universe (气)—manifestation of *Dao* as *Qi* during the restoration of the *Yin-Yang* balance.

Exhaustive—complete, all-inclusive, and comprehensive in reference to the mind, sensory reality, and their interaction. Nemonik thinking is an exhaustive way of thinking that includes all options. See Nemonik thinking.

Existence (有)—everything that we can perceive in the sensory reality. Existence and Non-existence were created during the first division of the Way (*Dao*) in its manifestation of Nothingness or Oneness. Existence is the complementary opposite of Non-existence. Nothingness is the absence of both Existence and Non-existence. Neither Existence nor Non-existence can be nothingness on its own. They need each other to recreate Nothingness.

External reality—material and immaterial phenomena that surround the mind. The external reality comprises the sensory and extrasensory realities. The extrasensory reality comprises the scientific and supernatural realities. The subconscious creates the internal, constructed, or simulated reality from the external reality.

Extrasensory reality—part of the external reality that cannot be perceived through the natural human senses. The extrasensory reality comprises the scientific and supernatural realities. See External reality.

Father of the Multitude (众父)—metaphor for the Way (*Dao*). See *Dao*.

First division—division of Oneness or Nothingness (*Dao*) in the Two. Oneness or Nothingness is the manifestation of the Way (*Dao*) as the undivided void of desolate emptiness, while the Two are Existence and Non-existence. In terms of mathematics, the first division could be written as: $0 = (+1) + (-1)$. The first division might have been what scientists describe as the Big Bang. See Second division and Third division.

Force—manifestation of the Way (*Dao*) as the unstoppable, neutral, and elusive power *Qi* that will harmonise each *Yin-Yang* balance.

Four Greatnesses (四大)—Lao Zi proposes that there are four Greatnesses in the Universe, which are in descending order *The Way, Sky, Earth, and King.* The King is a symbol for the people. Some might argue that Lao Zi proposes five entities, with nature representing the highest one. However, the Way (*Dao*) and nature are the same. Lao Zi does not mention divine power as one of the four Greatnesses. His Greatnesses are physical entities, rather than divine or spiritual ones.

Four stages of the formation: See Three stages of the formation.

Frugality (啬)—economic moderation that avoids extreme spending or wasting resources. As they say Waste *not, want not!* Frugality is one of Lao Zi's three treasures. He points out that there can be no generosity without frugality. Frugality does apply to both material and human resources. See Three treasures.

Genius—most able part of the mind that is hidden in the subconscious. See Subconscious.

Great Image (大象)—metaphor for the Way (*Dao*).

Great Road (大道)—metaphor for the Way (*Dao*).

Greatnesses (大)—See Four Greatnesses.

Greed—accumulation for the sake of accumulation. As they say—*Some know the price of everything and the value of nothing*. Greed causes unnecessary material imbalances and, therefore, it is likely to evoke counterproductive social friction. See Accumulate.

Guilford, Joy Paul (1897-1987)—US psychologist who developed Guilford's cube and introduced the concepts of convergent and divergent thinking. See Creative mindmode.

Harmonisation (相)—automatic process of maintaining and restoring the *Yin-Yang* balance by the Way (*Dao*). The Way is bound to maintain the cosmological constancy of Nothingness and, therefore it has to harmonise the *Yin-Yang* balance. Harmonisation is the constant of the Universe. During the process of harmonisation, the Way is often detectable by our senses as *Qi*. After each harmonisation, the Way will be undetectable again and return to Nothingness.

Harmony or tranquillity—temporary state of balance between *Yin* and *Yang* when the Way (*Dao*) is dormant.

Hierarchy of the Universe—See Four Greatnesses.

Humility(不敢为(天下)先)—*"not daring to become the world's first"* is mental moderation that avoids arrogance. Humility is a prerequisite for the ability to align with harmonisations of the Way (*Dao*) and one of Lao Zi three treasures. Humility is knowing and accepting our place, which is the lowest in the hierarchy of the Universe. See Three treasures.

Immortal Valley Spirit (谷神不死)—metaphor for the Way (*Dao*).

Incompetence (不善)—opposing the Way (*Dao*) and perishing as a result. People do not perish because they are evil, but because they are incompetent.

Inferior virtue (下德)—synonym for artificial virtue.

Interaction—effect of the mind on reality and vice versa. Whatever you do affects reality, while reality affects you. Reality is like a mirror that reflects your behaviour, which is called *'karma'*. The exhaustive components of interaction are *perception* and *projection*. Information management controls the flow of incoming and outgoing information. See Nemonik thinking.

Interactive nemoniks—nemoniks that deal with the interaction between the mind and reality. The four interactive nemoniks are *accept, reject, reveal, and conceal*. See Interaction.

Interception—ability to integrate the dimensions of space, time and matter that underlies our ability to catch and escape material objects.

Internal reality—subjective spatial, material, and temporal conscious perception of the external reality that is created by the subconscious. People perceive their internal reality as the true reality. However, the internal reality is subjective, because not everyone's perception and interpretation of the external reality is the same. Consequently, your internal reality might differ from the true external reality. See External reality.

Jing (經)—means literally *'classic'*. Therefore, *Dao De Jing* is a classic book in terms of the Chinese literature. *Jing* is a phonetic notation of a Chinese pictograph and, therefore, it is alternatively spelled as *Ching*.

Justice (义)—artificial Confucian virtue that maintains imbalances in the collective. As history shows, extreme imbalances in the distribution of wealth, status, privileges and power ultimately leads to violent social struggles. When this happens, the wealthy and powerful usually call for *'justice'* in order to protect the imbalances that advantage them. Their kind of justice often results in the maintenance of the status quo by increasing law and order. Under the pretence of stabilising the collective, the powerful use force to defend social inequalities. See Collective mindmode.

Karma—repayment for your actions. In Lao Zi's philosophy, the immutable Nothingness is divided during the First division in Existence and Non-existence. Nothingness cannot be changed and, therefore, Existence cannot change. Hence, the Way (*Dao*) in its manifestation of *Qi* is forced to harmonize all *Yin-Yang* balances. Consequently, if our actions disturb such a balance then *Qi* will restore that balance.

King (王)—lowest of the four Greatnesses that constitute the Universe. *"The Sky is great; the Earth is great; and the King is also great" (Lao Zi)*. The King is a symbol for the people, because Lao Zi replaces subsequently King (王) with people (人): *"People follow the Earth; the Earth follows the Sky" (Lao Zi)*. See Four Greatnesses.

Knowledge (贤)—information about the sensory and extrasensory realities. Confucian artificial knowledge is about manmade rules, customs, rituals, laws, and regulations. On the other hand, Lao Zi rejects that artificial knowledge and advocates natural knowledge. Nemonik thinking synthesizes the Laozian natural knowledge (objective) with the Confucian artificial knowledge (collective). It also incorporates beliefs (reactive).

Known—See Spencer.

Koan—riddles used in Zen Buddhism, which have no rational solution. Each Koan forces Zen students to find non-rational solutions with subconscious Affectorial thinking. For example, a Zen master brings his hands together, while saying to a student *"This is the sound of two hands clapping. What is the sound of one hand clapping?"* The koan will make us think again, about what we have taken for granted. This process of questioning our beliefs with a different way of thinking may provide new insight in the illusion that we call reality. Koans are useful for nemonik thinking, because they foster subconscious affectorial thinking.

Lao Tzu—See Lao Zi.

Lao Zi (老子) (570-490 BC)—Chinese sage and philosopher who wrote about two-and-half thousand years ago the book *Dao De Jing*. Lao Zi was the first philosopher who made a distinction between objective and collective thinking. *Dao* (The Way of Nature) refers to objective thinking, while *De* (The Way of People) refers to collective thinking. Lao Zi advocated natural virtue and rejected the Confucian artificial virtue. Lao Zi's real name might have been Li Ehr, who was a historian in the state Chu. However, scholars disagree about the personal details of Lao Zi. The name Lao Zi is a phonetic notation of Chinese pictographs. Therefore, it is alternatively spelled as LaoZi, Laozi, Lao Zi, LaoTzu, Laotzu, Lao Tsu, LaoTsu, Laotsu, Lao Tse, LaoTse, Laotse, etc. See *Dao De Jing*.

Lateral thinking—way of creative thinking that reformulates problems and looks at them from different perspectives in order to find solutions. Edward de Bono introduced this way of thinking in his book *'Lateral Thinking' (1970)*. The opposite of lateral thinking is vertical or rational thinking. Lateral thinking is part of the creative mindmode of nemonik thinking. However, nemonik thinking is superior, because it provides an exhaustive prompting system for de Bono's lateral thinking. Nemonik thinking is exhaustive and, therefore, the seventeen nemoniks provide all the possible perspectives to reformulate the actual problem. Each nemonik prompts the creative mindmode to generate questions and ideas from a different point of view. Hence, the nemonik template is a questions and ideas generator that adds process and structure to lateral thinking. See Creative mindmode.

Ma Wang Dui (马王堆)—tomb of a nobleman at Ma Wang Dui in Chang Sha, south-central China. Dating from 168 BC and unearthed in 1973, the tomb contained two copies of Lao Zi's *Dao De Jing* that are now known as the Ma Wang Dui texts A and B. The tomb acted as a time-capsule and revealed crucial information about the true meaning of *Dao De Jing*. Ma Wang Dui is a phonetic notation of Chinese pictographs and, therefore, it is alternatively spelled as Mawangdui, Ma Wang tui, or Mawangtui. See *Dao De Jing*.

Maintaining the *Yin-Yang* balance—preventing that either *Yin* or *Yang* becomes so large that the imbalance evokes a natural harmonisation. Maintaining the *Yin-Yang* balance is the first of the three fundamental alignments with the Way *(Dao)*. The unstoppable Way, in its manifestation of *Qi*, will always harmonise the *Yin-Yang* balance, because it has to maintain the cosmological constancy of Nothingness. Therefore, sages will maintain the *Yin-Yang* balances, because it is a waste of time and effort to disturb them.

Master Carpenter (大匠)—metaphor for the Way *(Dao)*.

Material—refers to matter.

Matter—three-dimensional finite part of reality that features substance, volume, and weight, and occupies and moves through space and time. Matter is wrapped up energy that is determined by four features: density, volume, shape, and motion. Matter is part of the sensory reality. Matter is organic or inorganic and includes resources such as animals, energy, equipment, information, money, people, plants, raw materials, etc. Einstein's formula $E = mc^2$ shows that energy (E) is another manifestation of matter (m). Information is classified as matter, because there is no information without matter. Matter provides the exhaustive options to *Accumulate, Preserve, and Dispose*. Transformation is a combination of accumulation and disposing matter. See Sensory reality.

Mental nemoniks—nemoniks that refer to a particular mindmode. They are the *objective, collective, creative, and reactive mindmode*. See Nemonik thinking.

Mindmode—specific way of thinking that deals with a specific aspect of the external reality. They comprise the *objective, collective, creative, and reactive mindmodes.* Each mindmode is an elementary way of thinking that has evolved as a result of natural environmental pressure. They are defined by different interactions between the order and chaos of the mental process versus the order and chaos of reality. (1) The objective mindmode uses mental order to deal with the natural order of reality. (2) The collective mindmode uses mental order to deal with the artificial order of reality. (3) The creative mindmode uses mental disorganization or chaos to deal with the chaos of reality. (4) The reactive mindmode uses mental order to deal with the chaos of reality. See Mind.

Mind—nonmaterial part of a person that comprises the total of all conscious, subconscious, and semiconscious mental structures and processes. The mind is abstract and can only exist in the extrasensory reality, because you cannot see, hear, taste, smell, or touch the mind. The mind is a theoretical construct that exists paradoxically in the mind. Nevertheless, this elusive construct helps us to evaluate our way of thinking. A healthy mind has a will, purpose, or intent that maintains goals such as maximizing success, obtaining comfort, escaping discomfort, and sustaining survival. Furthermore, it has abilities to think and memorize, and to maintain a productive interaction with the external reality. The mind has to deal with the order and chaos of reality. Therefore, the mind generates respectively rational thinking and affectorial thinking. Rational thinking is divided in the objective and collective mindmodes, while affectorial thinking is divided in the creative and reactive mindmodes. Concentration fosters conscious dominance and rational thinking. On the other hand, relaxation fosters subconscious dominance and affectorial thinking. See Nemonik thinking.

Mindsets—internalized sets of rules that are derived by the reactive mindmode from the past, the known, or experience in order to generate reactive affecters. Initially, mindsets are created by your conscious and stored in your subconscious. Every repetitive action or thought becomes ultimately a mindset. The reactive mindmode generates mindsets through the process of habituation. In computer science, mindsets could be compared to algorithms. The aim of mindsets is to increase our speed and accuracy of our decisions and actions by using pre-programmed instructions. The application of mindsets requires subconscious dominance or a silent mind. The mindsets are honed each time they are used. After each improvement, there is less need for conscious interference and the mindset sinks deeper into our subconscious. A disadvantage is the rigidity of the action or thoughts evoked by a mindset. See Reactive mindmode.

Moderation (无极)—avoiding extreme values of either *Yin* or *Yang*.

Mother (母)—metaphor for the Way (*Dao*).

Mysterious Female (玄牝)—metaphor for the Way (*Dao*).

Named (名)—divided manifestation of the Way (*Dao*).

Nameless (无名)—undivided manifestation of the Way as the Oneness or Simplicity.

Naming or Being Named (有名)—process of dividing entities in parts. After something is divided into smaller parts, we need names in order to differentiate these parts from each other. In Lao Zi's philosophy, naming is the illusionary division of the Way (*Dao*). The division of the Way is illusionary, because the Way is the Oneness, which cannot really be divided. Lao Zi's idea is similar to ideas in quantum mechanics.

Natural virtue—competence to align with the Way of nature (*Dao*). It is the competence to be in the right place, at the right time, with the right resources, and in the right frame of mind. The Way is objective and eternal. Therefore, virtue that is based upon the Way is also objective and eternal. The unstoppable Way is the highest Greatness in the hierarchy of the Universe. Hence, natural virtue or Laozian virtue (objective) is superior to artificial or Confucian virtue, which is based on temporary manmade rules. See *Dao De Jing*.

Nemonik template—basis for nemonik thinking, which comprises the seventeen nemoniks. The template is a checklist to evaluate the actual situation or problem. Each nemonik could be evaluated with the SWOT-analysis. See Nemonik thinking.

Nemonik thinking—exhaustive and systematic way of thinking that maximizes the probability of success by subjecting seventeen nemoniks to both rational and affectorial thinking. The supernatural is outside the scope of nemonik thinking. Thinking is a self-organizing mental process that recalls, evaluates, transforms, and generates information. Exhaustive means complete, all-inclusive, comprehensive, and every possibility included in reference to the mind, sensory reality, and the interaction between the mind and reality. Nemonik thinking is dynamic because it adjusts efficiently to changes in the sensory reality. Nemonik thinking is systematic and, therefore, it is the first teachable way of thinking. Rational thinking is a conscious way of thinking that is associated with logic and reason. Affectorial thinking is a subconscious way of thinking associated with creativity, beliefs, intuitions, and emotions. Nemonik thinking is unique, easy to learn and simple to use. It mobilizes your hidden genius, accelerates your thinking, improves your memory, reveals opportunities and threats, creates questions and ideas, and reduces your stress levels. The prime aim of nemonik thinking is maximizing the probability of success. *Success is to obtain what you seek and escape what you suffer (Lao Zi)*.

Nemoniks—memorized keywords describing the exhaustive aspects of the mind, reality, and the interaction of the mind and reality, which prompt the memory to recall associated information. The word nemonik is a phonetic notation of the Greek word mnemonic, which means *memory aid*. In accord, nemoniks improve your thinking by defragmenting your memory and prompting your memory to recall information. However, nemoniks are more than plain mnemonics. Nemoniks are also mental tools for guiding your thinking, consciously managing your larger subconscious, activating your subconscious to generate ideas and reveal intuitions, and building tactics and strategies. Furthermore, the constant readiness of the nemoniks is expected to reduce your anxiety and stress levels. The four mental nemoniks include the *objective, collective, creative, and the reactive mindmodes*. The nine reality nemoniks include *advance, stay, retreat, accumulate, preserve, dispose, act, wait, and prepare*. The four interactive nemoniks include *accept, reject, reveal, and conceal*. The thirteen operational nemoniks include the nine reality nemoniks and four interactive nemoniks. Best of all, you do not have to worry nemonik thinking, because the nemoniks will be habituated automatically by your subconscious. Ultimately, nemonik thinking is like playing a musical keyboard with seventeen keys producing an infinite repertoire of strategies to deal with the sensory reality. See Nemonik thinking.

Newton, Sir Isaac (1642-1727)—British mathematician and physicists who described in his book *Principia* some of the basic laws of nature. Einstein synthesized Newton's thesis that light comprised small particles with Young's antithesis that light was a wave.

Non-action (无为)—means literally action *'without action'*. The principle of Non-action entails an efficient use of the unlimited force of the Way so that sages achieve their goals with a minimum of effort and resources. It does not mean that sages are lazy, passive, or fatalistic. Sages have to be alert and time their actions to align themselves with the Way. For instance, one could travel in leisure by using sails, rather than using depleting one's strength with rowing.

Non-existence (无有)—cannot be perceived and is diametrically opposed to Existence. Non-existence and Existence were created during the first division of the Way (*Dao*) in its manifestation of Nothingness. Existence is the complementary opposite of Non-existence. Nothingness is the absence of both Existence and Non-existence. Neither Existence nor Non-existence can be nothingness on its own. They need each other to recreate Nothingness. Lao Zi's concept of Non-existence is not just the absence of existence. It is less than nothing—it is a shortage of existence. Lao Zi's idea of Non-existence might be similar to the modern idea of antimatter. See First division.

Nothingness(无物)—manifestation of the Way (*Dao*) as the undivided void of desolate emptiness that was the origin of the Universe. Nothingness is devoid of substance and is ultimately inconceivable. Nothingness is the true constant of the Cosmos that cannot be decreased or increased. During the first division, Nothingness was divided into Non-existence and Existence. Nothingness is the sum and absence of both Existence and Non-existence. See First division.

Objective mindmode—way of rational thinking that deals with the natural order of the sensory reality, which can be described by natural laws and facts that make nature predictable. Objective refers to a description of reality that is independent of what anyone believes. The objective mindmode is a conscious way of thinking that is activated by concentration.—In contrast to the collective mindmode, the objective mindmode pertains to the laws of nature. In contrast to the creative mindmode, the objective mindmode will increase our knowledge step-by-step in an incremental way.—The objective mindmode uses the mental order of reason to deal with the natural order of reality. Objective thinking generates science. Sir Isaac Newton was the one of the first scientists to describe objectively the laws of the sensory reality. Albert Einstein and Max Planck extended Newton's ideas into the extrasensory reality. Objective specialists are found where proficiency in natural laws is crucial such as in science and technology. See Rational thinking.

One(一)—manifestation of the Way (*Dao*) as the indivisible or nameless entity that comprises our Existence. See First division and Second division.

Operational nemoniks—thirteen nemoniks comprising the nine reality nemoniks and the four interactive nemoniks. See Nemoniks.

Origin of the Universe—See Nothingness.

People (民)—See King.

Perception—part of the nemonik interaction that manages the incoming information flow from the sensory reality towards the mind. The senses facilitate sensory perception by detecting incoming information. The exhaustive options provided by perception for maximizing success are to *Accept and Reject* information. Listening is an easy way to gain information. See Interaction.

Planck, Max (1858-1947)—German theoretical physicist who introduced in 1900 quantum mechanics, which is concerned with infinitesimal subatomic phenomena outside the sensory reality, which are called quanta.

Positioning—ability to manoeuvre into a situation where the strategic advantage is so large that the opposition has to avoid a conflict at all cost. Sun Zi warns against rash actions: 'Competent generals do not fight'. Any conflict will destroy resources on both sides. Therefore, a superior general positions his army into a situation where the strategical advantage is so large that his opponent will avoid a battle. In that way, the general uses resources more effectively, prevent mutual destruction, minimise negative feelings and acquire new resources that are not damaged by conflict. See The Art of War and Prepare.

Prepare—temporal nemonik that prompts the mind to get ready for action. Preparation includes analysing, decision-making, learning, mind management, negotiating, organizing, planning, positioning, prioritizing, risk-management, fostering leadership, setting goals, internalizing nemonik thinking, time management, training, etc. Preparation is productive if it is based on proactivity, while it is counterproductive if it is used as an excuse for procrastination. The 80/20 rule supports the notion that perfect preparation is counterproductive. Even imperfect things and actions might be extremely useful. See Time.

Preserve—material nemonik that prompts the mind to maintain the same amount of matter that is under control. See Matter.

Principle of the Universe—the Way (*Dao*), in its manifestation of *Qi*, will always harmonise the *Yin-Yang* balance, because it has to maintain the cosmological constancy of Nothingness.

Procrastination—counterproductive delay of action that inhibits opportunities and fosters threats. See Time.

Productive harmonisations—harmonisations of the *Yin-Yang* balance by the Way (*Dao*) that foster success. Beneficial would be a subjective label, because all harmonisations are neutral. We conceive them only as being either counterproductive or productive in relation to our personal success. See Harmonisation.

Projection—part of interaction that refers to managing the outgoing information flow from the mind towards the sensory reality. The exhaustive options provided by projection for maximizing success are to *Reveal and Conceal* information. See Interaction.

Propriety (礼)—artificial Confucian virtue that entails conformity to the system of rules and beliefs that maintain a society. Propriety tells us the way that things should and ought to be done. Propriety explains with collective arguments why it is proper to have socio-economic differences in the collective. Propriety is so deeply hidden in the soul that only young rebels (unconditioned) dare question its validity.

Qi (气) or vital energy—manifestation of the Way (*Dao*) as the neutral force that will always harmonise the *Yin-Yang* balance in order to maintain the constant Nothingness. *Qi* is elusive and can hide in matter. It is only detectable when it restores the *Yin-Yang* balance. The energy of *Qi* is vital for all life, but it is neither good nor evil.

Rashness—fast but counterproductive decisions without adequate conscious thoughts or subconscious mindsets. Rashness stops the conflict between the conscious and subconscious for mental dominance, because the dice are thrown. Hence, rashness is often a counterproductive attempt to avoid or stop a panic attack. See Reactive mindmode.

Rational thinking—conscious part of nemonik thinking that deals with the predictable order of reality by submitting facts to reason in order to create new facts. Rational thinking uses the mental order of reason to deal with the order of the sensory reality. The mental processes underlying rational thinking are within the conscious awareness, and therefore, they can be observed directly. Rational thinking comprises critical thinking that fosters distrust and emotional detachment. Concentration fosters conscious dominance and rational thinking. Rational thinking comprises the objective and collective mindmodes. In Lao Zi's philosophy, rational thinking could be called *Yang* thinking. See Conscious.

Reactive affecters—affecters that are generated by mindsets and deal with the chaos of reality. They include beliefs, common sense, desires, emotions, feelings, habits, heuristics, impulses, intuitions, reactions, reflexes, routines, sensibilities, skills, etc. See Reactive mindmode.

Reactive mindmode—way of affectorial thinking that deals with the chaos of reality by habituating mindsets that generate reactive affecters. Reactive affecters include beliefs, common sense, desires, emotions, habits, heuristics, impulses, informal logic, intuitions, reactions, reflexes, routines, sensibility, skills, etc. The reactive mindmode uses mental preparation or order to deal with the chaos of reality. It is the aim of the reactive mindmode to optimize your mental and physical perfection. However, the reactive mindmode is a product of the past. It relies on your experience and, therefore, it keeps you within your comfort zone. The Chinese philosopher Lao Zi advocated reactive thinking. Reactive specialists are found where individual perfection is crucial such as in chess, driving, martial arts, sports, surgery, etc. See Affectorial thinking.

Reality—See External reality.

Reject—perceptual nemonik that prompts the mind to refuse the incoming information as a true description of the sensory reality. See Perception.

Restoring the *Yin-Yang* balance—artificial process of restoring the *Yin-Yang* balance by people in order to defuse natural but counterproductive harmonisations by the Way (*Dao*). It is the third of the three fundamental alignments with the Way. The crucial imbalances in our environment that are caused by *Yang* technology and rational or *Yang* thinking demonstrate the importance of this fundamental alignment. We may have to defuse the potentially counterproductive harmonisations before they gain more momentum. Industrial pollution is a prime example.

Retreat—spatial nemonik that prompts the mind to increase the distance to the goal. See Space.

Reveal—projectional nemonik that prompts the mind to project true information to the sensory reality. See Projection.

River (川)—metaphor for the Way (*Dao*).

Sages (圣人)—wise people who align with the Natural Way (*Dao*) by fostering natural virtue (*De*). They are in the right place, at the right time, with the right resources and in the right frame of mind. On the other hand, Confucian sages align with the Artificial Way of the People by fostering artificial virtues. The term sage may refer to man and woman alike.

Scientific reality—part of the extrasensory reality that can be perceived with artificial sensors or rational thinking. See External reality.

Second division—formation of the Universe as the result of the interaction between Existence and Non-Existence, which creates the Three Greatnesses. The Three Greatnesses are: The Sky, the Earth, and the King or the People. Subsequently, these Three Greatnesses generate All-things that are the myriad of organic and non-organic things in our Universe. See First division and Third division.

Semiconscious—part of the mind that comprises parts of the conscious and subconscious, which form a communication channel between those parts of the mind. The semiconscious is associated with dream awareness, meditation, hypnosis, and drowsiness. See Mind.

Senses—integrated physiological and mental systems that perceive material signals from the sensory reality and transform them into neural signals. The five traditional senses are hearing, seeing, smelling, tasting, and touching. However, people have also senses for balance, body position, movement, pain, pressure, temperature, etc. See Perception.

Sensors—cells in the body that are able to detect sensory signals from the sensory reality and convert them into nerve signals. See Senses.

Sensory reality—part of the external reality that can be perceived directly through the natural human senses. If not otherwise indicated, *reality* means *sensory reality*. Lorenz emphasized the difference between the deterministic order and chaotic parts of reality. However, acquiring facts transforms chaos into order. Hence, the distinction between order and chaos depends on the development of one's mind, rather than on the features of the external reality. Therefore, that distinction is subjective, rather than objective. Organizing and disorganizing transform reality. The mind has developed different ways to deal with the order of reality (consciously) and chaos of reality (subconsciously). See External reality.

Simplicity (朴)—synonym for the Way (*Dao*). It is the undivided manifestation of the Way as Oneness or Nameless that is often called the uncarved or wooden block.

Sky (天)—second of the Four Greatnesses that constitute the Universe.

Space—three-dimensional, infinite, and nonmaterial part of reality in which matter is immersed and moves around. Space provides the exhaustive options to *Advance, Stay, and Retreat*. See Sensory reality.

Spatial—refers to space.

Spencer, Herbert (1820-1903)—English philosopher who introduced the important distinctions between the known, unknown, and unknowable. The creative mindmode deals with the unknown, while the reactive mindmode deals with the known. The unknowable is part of the supernatural reality and is therefore excluded from nemonik thinking. See Nemonik thinking.

Ssu-ma Ch'ien (c. 145-86 BC)—Chinese historian who compiled the *Shih Chi* or Historical Records, which comprised the first comprehensive history of China. Allegedly, Ssu-ma Ch'ien refers to Lao Zi as Li Ehr.

Stay—spatial nemonik that prompts the mind to maintain the same distance to the goal. See Space.

Straw dogs (刍狗)—metaphor for non-action. Straw dogs have excellent qualities in Lao Zi's philosophy. If people would act as straw dogs, they would not act at all. In that case, they align with the Way (*Dao*) by following the crucial principle of Non-action. Even sages will apply the principle of Non-action as if they were straw dogs. Hence, Lao Zi's remark about straw dogs is not demeaning in the context of *Dao De Jing*.

Subconscious—large part of the mind that is continuously active outside the conscious awareness of that person. The subconscious is associated with sleep, relaxation, knowledge, genius, internal reality, and affectorial thinking. The prime aim of the subconscious is to protect the conscious from an information overload. The resulting mental silence allows the conscious to direct and manage the subconscious. The acquisition of information and creation of mindsets cost much time and effort. Therefore, whether correct or incorrect, subconscious information is precious. Consequently, the subconscious has to protect the acquired information against opposing information. However, this protection of the subconscious could cause close mindedness, cognitive dissonance, extremism, groupthink, and mental stagnation. The subconscious generates affectorial thinking. See Mind.

Substance of the Universe—Existence is the substance of our Universe. Non-existence is useful, because it maintains this substance.

Success—*obtain what you seek and escape what you suffer (Lao Zi)*. Some people might seek fame, freedom, knowledge, power, safety, skills, wealth, etc. Others will try to escape ignorance, obscurity, oppression, poverty, violence, weakness, etc. Some might even denounce all desires. Nevertheless, each goal would fit Lao Zi's definition of success. Hence, it is the aim of a healthy mind to maximize success, while survival is the first step of that success. However, incompetent thinkers set the wrong goals and, therefore, they obtain what they suffer most and escape what they need most. The aim of nemonik thinking is maximizing the probability of success. Therefore, nemonik thinking is goal oriented and fosters compassion, allies, and win-win strategies. In contrast, the aim of conventional thinking is maximizing the probability of winning. See Winning.

Sum-zero-creation—creation in which the sum of all the parts remains zero. In Lao Zi's philosophy, before the formation of the Universe, there was only the Way (*Dao*) in its manifestation of Nothingness. Nothing could be added to it or subtracted from it during the formation, simply because there was nothing else. Therefore, Nothingness remained the same after its division into Existence and Non-existence. Hence, the sum of Existence and Non-existence can only recreate Nothingness. See First division.

Sun Zi (554-496 BC)—Chinese warrior-philosopher who wrote about two-and-half thousand years ago the book—*Bingfa or The Art of War*. Scholars disagree about the personal details of Sun Zi. His real name might have been Sunwu. The name Sun Zi is a phonetic notation of

Chinese pictographs and, therefore, his name is alternatively spelled as SunZi, Sunzi, Sun Tsu, SunTzu, Suntzu, Sun Tse, Suntse, Sun Wu, SunWu, Sunwu, etc. See The Art of War.

Superior virtue (上德)—synonym for Lao Zi's Natural virtue.

Supernatural reality—part of the extrasensory reality that is outside the scientific reality. The supernatural reality includes such phenomena as clairvoyance, divine power, ESP, extrasensory perception, God, paranormal, precognition, PSI, psychokinesis, spirit, telekinesis, and telepathy. The supernatural reality is associated with Spencer's concept of the *unknowable*. The supernatural is outside the scope of nemonik thinking. See External reality.

Tao Te Ching—See Dao De Jing.

Taoism—See Daoism.

Tao—See Dao.

The Art of War or Bing Fa—book about strategy written by Sun Zi about two-and-half thousand years ago. Although written about war, Sun Zi's advice applies also to daily life. *Bing Fa* is a phonetic notation of Chinese pictographs and, therefore, it is alternatively spelled as Bingfa, Pingfa, Ping Fa, etc. See Appendix.

Theory of the Cosmos—Lao Zi's cosmological theory holds that during the first division, the nameless void of desolate empty Nothingness (*Dao*) was simultaneously divided into Existence and Non-existence. Existence and Non-existence are equal but opposing polarities and, therefore their sum can only recreate Nothingness or zero. This sum-zero-creation might underlie a supersymmetry in which each participle or force has a mirror particle or force of an equal magnitude and opposing polarity. See Sum-zero creation.

Thinking—self-organizing mental process that recalls, evaluates, transforms, and generates information. The quality of your thinking determines your education, mental and physical wellbeing, socio-economic status, and the overall quality and duration of your life. It determines whether you are at war or live in peace. Your thinking determines everything worth living for. See Nemonik thinking.

Third division—division of the Three into All-things. In Lao Zi's philosophy, the Three are: The Sky, the Earth and the King or the people. Together they create All-things, which are the myriad of organic and inorganic things that exist in the sensory reality. See First division and Second division.

Three (三)—refers to the three Greatnesses of the second division of the formation of the Universe: The Sky, the Earth and the King or the people. See *Dao De Jing*.

Three fundamental alignments—Maintaining the *Yin-Yang* balance; Aligning with Harmonisations; and Restoring the *Yin-Yang* balance (Lao Zi). These fundamental alignments were derived from the possible options of sages to align with the Way (*Dao*). See Maintaining the *Yin-Yang* balance, Aligning with harmonisations, Restoring the *Yin-Yang* balance.

Three stages of the formation—Oneness is the manifestation of the Way (*Dao*) as the Nameless void of desolate empty Nothingness, which is the origin of the Universe (Lao Zi). We may reduce Lao Zi's four stages of the formation of the Universe to three: *"The One generated the Two; the Two generated the Three; and the Three generated All-things."*

Three treasures (三宝)—frugality, humility and compassion (Lao Zi). Maintaining the *Yin-Yang* balance includes frugality; Aligning with the harmonisations includes humility and Restoring the *Yin-Yang* balance

Time—one-dimensional, eternal, and nonmaterial part of reality that can be perceived indirectly by changes in matter and the movement of matter through space. Time provides the exhaustive nemoniks to *Act, Wait, and Prepare*. See Sensory reality.

Timing—execution of an action at the most productive moment. See Time.

Tranquillity (靜)—See Harmony.

Treasures—See Three treasures.

Two (二)—refers to Existence and Non-existence (Lao Zi). Those were generated during the first division of the formation of the Universe. Incorrectly, some have explained that the Two refers to *Yin* and *Yang*. However, *Yin* and *Yang* are associated with All-things, which is the lowest entity in the hierarchy of the formation of the Universe. See Second division.

Uncarved block—See Simplicity.

Unconsciousness—unhealthy mental state that is characterized by a persistent unawareness of the sensory reality and the Self. Unconsciousness differs from subconscious dominance, because you will not wake up in case of danger. Hence, unconsciousness could be seen as a suspension of life. Unconsciousness could be caused by physical or mental traumas, analgesics, asphyxiation, and toxic substances. See Mind.

Universe (国)—that part of Nothingness or Cosmos, which forms the sensory reality comprising matter, space and time. The Universe of our reality is created by the division of Nothingness into Existence and Non-existence (Lao Zi). It is not excluded that there is also a parallel or anti-Universe that comprises negative matter, space, and time. *Universe'* seems to be a more appropriate interpretation of (国) than *'country'*.

Valley (谷)—metaphor for the Way.

Virtue—See *De*.

Vital energy—See *Qi*.

Void—See Nothingness.

Wait—temporal nemonik that prompts the mind to delay an action until it is the right time for that action. See Time.

Water (水)—metaphor for the Way (*Dao*).

Way—See *Dao*.

Winning—defeating opponents in competition and, therefore, winning is conflict oriented, which fosters control, force, aggression, enemies, and win-lose strategies. The aim of conventional thinking is maximizing the probability of winning. In contrast, the aim of nemonik thinking is maximizing the probability of success. See Success.

MY OTHER BOOKS

LAO ZI'S DAO DE JING

(Schade, Lao Zi's True Dao De Jing, planned 2017) contains unique Chinese and English versions of Lao Zi's *Dao De Jing*, which means—*The Way of Nature and the Way of People*. Lao Zi was a Chinese philosopher who lived during the 6th century BC but is still ahead of our time. His brilliance outshines intellectual giants such as Confucius, Sun Zi, Socrates, Plato, and Aristotle. Lao Zi's aim is achieving success, which is to *obtain what you seek and escape what you suffer*. Success is achieved by aligning the *Way of People* with the *Way of Nature*. Lao Zi's success is secular and based on competence, rather than devotion. It is about positioning, rather than competing. Lao Zi's deep understanding of nature and people is crucial for your immediate survival and that of the next generation. Humanity is facing overpopulation, dwindling resources, nuclear warfare, pollution, climate change, etc. We cannot solve those problems with the same way of thinking that is causing them. The brutal reality shows that our way of thinking is failing. Therefore, Lao Zi's eternal wisdom is the guiding light for our future. Its simplicity reaches peacefully across the boundaries of race, religion, spiritualism, ideology, and science.

LAO TZU'S TAO TE CHING

(Schade, Lao Tzu's Tao Te Ching, 2016) is an abridged English-only version of (Schade, Lao Zi's Dao De Jing, 2016), which means—*The Way of Nature and the Way of People*. Lao Zi was a Chinese philosopher who lived during the 6th century BC but is still ahead of our time. His brilliance outshines intellectual giants such as Confucius, Sun Zi, Socrates, Plato, and Aristotle. Lao Zi's aim is to teach success, which is to *obtain what you seek and escape what you suffer*. Success is achieved by aligning the *Way of People* with the *Way of Nature*. Lao Zi's success is secular and based on competence, rather than devotion. It is about positioning, rather than competing. Lao Zi's deep understanding of nature and people is crucial for your immediate survival and that of the next generation. We are facing overpopulation, dwindling resources, nuclear warfare, pollution, climate change, etc. We cannot solve those problems with the same way of thinking that is causing them. The brutal reality shows that our way of thinking is failing. Therefore, Lao Zi's eternal wisdom is the guiding light for our future. Its simplicity reaches peacefully across the boundaries of race, religion, spiritualism, ideology, and science.

LAO ZI META-TRANSLATION

(Schade, Lao Zi's Dao De Jing: Meta-translation, 2016).

Lao Zi's eternal wisdom shines through in the numerous English translations of his *Dao De Jing*. Nevertheless, comparisons show that some individual Chinese pictographs and their interpretations are unclear. Therefore, this meta-translation is based on seven reputable Chinese versions. In order to select the most reliable pictographs, each one was compared across all versions. As changes might have occurred over time, the chance of a pictograph being included depended on the age of the version in which it appears. The consistent use of each pictograph was enhanced by computer assisted comparisons across the entire text. In addition, ten reputable English translations were synthesized in order to extract an initial context for each pictograph. The selected pictographs were translated with

(Schade, Lao Zi's Dao De Jing: Chinese-English Dictionary, planned 2017) that was compiled for this purpose. The guiding principle for this meta-translation has been the core of Lao Zi's philosophy—*The One generated the Two*. The importance of that sentence is explained in (Schade, Lao Zi's Dao De Jing Explained, 2016).

LAO ZI EXPLAINED

(Schade, Lao Zi's Dao De Jing Explained, 2016).

For more than two and a half thousand years, *Dao De Jing* has been shrouded in mystery. The poetic beauty of Lao Zi's words has maintained its dazzling shine that hides his esoteric secrets. In accord, Lao Zi wrote—*My words are very easy to understand and very easy to apply. Yet, people cannot understand them and they cannot apply them.* Many scholars have attempted unsuccessfully to peel away layer after layer of meaning to unravel its cryptic secrets. In contrast, the present book reveals Lao Zi's secret teachings for the first time in a clearly understandable way, imparting hidden knowledge about the *Way of Nature* and the *Way of People*. The core of Lao Zi's teachings is success, which is—*obtaining what you seek and escaping what you suffer.* Success is secular and based on competence, rather than devotion. It is about positioning, rather than competing. It is achieved by aligning the *Way of People* with the *Way of Nature*. The guiding principle for the present explanation is the core of Lao Zi's philosophy—*The One generated the Two.* Humanity is facing huge manmade problems with a failing way of thinking. Therefore, Lao Zi's eternal wisdom is more relevant than ever.

LAO ZI DICTIONARY

(Schade, Lao Zi's Dao De Jing: Chinese-English Dictionary, planned 2017).

Lao Zi's manuscript is more than 2,500 years old, while most Chinese-English dictionaries focus on the modern meaning of Chinese pictographs. Therefore, this special dictionary was compiled from several reputable public resources in order to get as close to the true meaning of each pictograph as possible. (Schade, Lao Zi's Dao De Jing: Meta-translation, 2016) is based on seven Chinese versions of *Dao De Jing*. Altogether, those versions comprise about 1,600 different pictographs, which are included in the present dictionary. Furthermore, this dictionary introduces a unique numerical coding system for Chinese pictographs that could improve the search method concerning hard copies of Chinese reference books.

Download a free eBook version
@ nemonik-thinking.org

NEMONIK THINKING

(Schade, Think Smarter with Nemonik Thinking, 2016). This is the operating manual for your mind that you should have received at birth. Nemonik thinking is a smarter way of thinking that aims to maximize your success by evaluating seventeen nemoniks, which are memorized keywords describing all the perceived aspects of your mind, reality, and their interaction. Success is obtaining what you seek and escaping what you suffer. To maximize that success, nemonik thinking mobilizes the hidden genius, accelerates thinking, improves memory, reveals opportunities and threats, creates questions and ideas, and reduces stress levels. It is like playing a musical keyboard with seventeen keys producing an infinite repertoire of smart strategies. Nemonik thinking is unique because it is the first exhaustive and transferable way of thinking. In contrast, conventional thinking is time consuming. Hence, the less time you have, the greater the necessity to study nemonik thinking. You might be the smartest thinker in the world, but only nemonik thinking could make you the smartest thinker you can be.

Download a free eBook version
@ nemonik-thinking.org

NEMONIK GLOSSARY

(Schade, Glossary Nemonik Thinking, 2016).

Nemonik thinking is a competitive advantage because it mobilizes the hidden genius, accelerates thinking, improves memory, prevents blind-spots, and reveals opportunities, while its constant preparedness reduces stress levels. Definitions, associated with the mind and reality, are inherently hypothetical, fuzzy, and intertwined. Nevertheless, to improve our understanding of the way we think, we have to identify, differentiate, and define those components. Therefore, this glossary provides descriptions for the concepts associated with nemonik thinking. To become skilled in nemonik thinking, it is recommended to study— (Schade, Think Smarter with Nemonik Thinking, 2016).

Download a free eBook version
@ nemonik-thinking.org

NEMONIK DICTIONARY

(Schade, Dictionary Nemonik Thinking, 2016).

Nemonik thinking mobilizes the hidden genius, accelerates thinking, improves memory, reveals opportunities and threats, creates questions and ideas, and reduces stress levels. Nemonik thinking divides the mind into 17 nemonik regions. That division defragments information, which facilitates the storage, maintenance, recall, and processing of associated information from memory. However, the boundaries of the nemonik regions are fuzzy. Therefore, the aim of this dictionary is to differentiate them by providing keywords for each nemonik concept. The first part of this dictionary translates nemonik concepts into common keywords e.g. *advance* into attack, bypass, etc. In contrast, the second part translates common keywords into nemonik concepts e.g. attack, bypass, etc. into *advance*. This dictionary shows that the complexity of conventional thinking comprises thousands of keywords that can be simplified to 17 nemoniks. This reduction will increase the speed of your thinking. To become skilled in nemonik thinking, it is recommended to study— (Schade, Think Smarter with Nemonik Thinking, 2016).

EDUCATION KILLS HUMANITY

(Schade, Education Kills Humanity, 2016).

Humanity is facing huge manmade problems such as overpopulation, dwindling resources, pollution, climate change, and warfare. Nevertheless, we should not blame corrupt politicians, uncaring industrialists, greedy investors, passionate greenies, and warmongers. They are the products of our educational system, which conditions students with ratings to maximize the probability of winning. Winning is defeating opponents in competition. Therefore, conventional thinking is conflict oriented, which fosters aggression, control, effort, and force. This inhibits the truth and, therefore, it is self-destructive. The educational failure is maintained by cognitive dissonance and groupthink. In contrast, nemonik thinking aims for success, which is to obtain what you seek and to escape what you suffer. Therefore, nemonik thinking is goal oriented, which fosters freedom, alignment, compassion, allies, and win-win strategies. You might be the smartest thinker in the world, but only nemonik thinking could make you the smartest thinker you can be. This manuscript is an abridged version of (Schade, Think Smarter with Nemonik Thinking, 2016).

GLOBAL WARMING

(Schade, Global Warming is the Solution, 2016).

This book presents a bilateral hypothesis for climate change. Mainstream climatology lacks scientific integrity and statistical methodology. Peer review is changed into peer pressure and objectors are silenced by labelling them *'Deniers'*. Proper statistical analyses are replaced by fancy graphs and non-causal correlation analyses. The conclusions are predominantly based on the last 166 years, while 420,000 years of Antarctic data are ignored. Climatology also ignores the solar expert Professor Zharkova, who predicts a mini ice-age by 2030. The present study shows that the current 400 ppm of CO_2 predicts a global temperature of 11.5 °C. It also shows that the observed global temperature of 1.3 °C failed to reach statistical significance. In addition, the data support the hypothesis that we live in a glacial period. This hypothesis is supported by the thermal gap of CO_2, the long interglacial duration, and the interglacial thermal stability. Consequently, decreasing atmospheric CO_2 could induce glacial conditions threatening the survival of humanity.

Download a free eBook version
@ nemonik-thinking.org

SUN ZI'S THE ART OF WAR

(Schade, Sun Zi's The Art of War, planned 2017).

Sun Zi (554-496 BC) was a Chinese warrior-philosopher who wrote the military classic *Bing Fa* or *The Art of War*. Although his book is about war, his strategies apply to every facet of daily life. Sun Zi deals with the art of positioning yourself in space, matter, and time. He addresses the questions raised by nemonik thinking of where, what, and when to advance, stay, retreat, accumulate, preserve, dispose, act, wait, prepare, accept, reject, reveal, and conceal. Think smarter and incorporate Sun Zi's strategies in your thinking. To become skilled in nemonik thinking, it is recommended to study— (Schade, Think Smarter with Nemonik Thinking, 2016).

Download a free eBook version
@ nemonik-thinking.org

WEBSITE

It is the aim of my website to provide interactive on-line information about nemonik thinking. This includes discussions, books, blog, videos, exercises, updates, activities, web links, and tests. Join the nemonik thinkers and receive the latest updates. It is a work in progress. Check it out and have your say! I look forward to your feedback at:

nemonik-thinking.org

ENDNOTES

[i] File: Word count.excell / Dao De Jing Structure /

[ii] In terms of arithmetic, the creation of the Universe could be written as: $0 = (+X) + (-X)$. In which: Nothingness = 0; Existence = +X; and Non-existence = -X.

[iii] For example; $1 + 2 = 3$. The equal sign (=) indicates that there is balance between the question ($1 + 2 = ?$) and the answer (= 3).

www.ingramcontent.com/pod-product-compliance
Lightning Source LLC
Chambersburg PA
CBHW070919180426
43192CB00038B/1868